The Journey of

Justus Falckner

(1672-1723)

Kim-Eric Williams

ALPB Books
Delhi, New York

Lutheran Archives Center at Philadelphia

Contents

To my parents
Paul Ellsworth Williams
and
Marjorie Elizabeth Talley Williams

*"Högt i stjarnehimlen kan vi dig ej finna,
men i manskovimlet är du bland oss Gud."*

Anders Frostenson
Den Svenska Psalmboken (1986), nr. 25

---

*With grateful acknowledgedment
for generous support
in publishing this book:*

In memory of
Pastor Willis D. Leece
by
Pastor Larry M. Neff
and
Pastor Frederick S. Weiser

In memory of
Pastor Charles D. Trexler, Jr.
by
Pastor Glenn C. Stone
and
Meredith Nordaas Stone

Foreword

This biography of a key figure in colonial Lutheranism is both timely and necessary. It is appropriate that, at the time of the 300th anniversary of his Ordination, Justus Falckner will finally get the attention he deserves.

Kim-Eric Williams has given us an account of Falckner's life that is straightforward and detailed.. The casual reader may not recognize that Williams is breaking new ground with virtually every chapter. Although Justus Falckner was the first Lutheran pastor to be ordained in the New World and then served a great swath of settlement in colonial New York, his story has been clouded in myth and conjecture. Now, relying on primary sources in several languages, Kim-Eric Williams leads us through Falckner's life from his birth in Germany to his death in the Hudson River valley.. This is truly a landmark publication.

Thanks are due to President George Handley and the Board of Directors of The Lutheran Archives Center at Philadelphia, who have sponsored this publication in cooperation with the Archives Advisory Committee of the Metropolitan New York Synod of the Evangelical Lutheran Church in America. May it edify and inspire us.

H. George Anderson
Presiding Bishop emeritus
Evangelical Lutheran Church in America

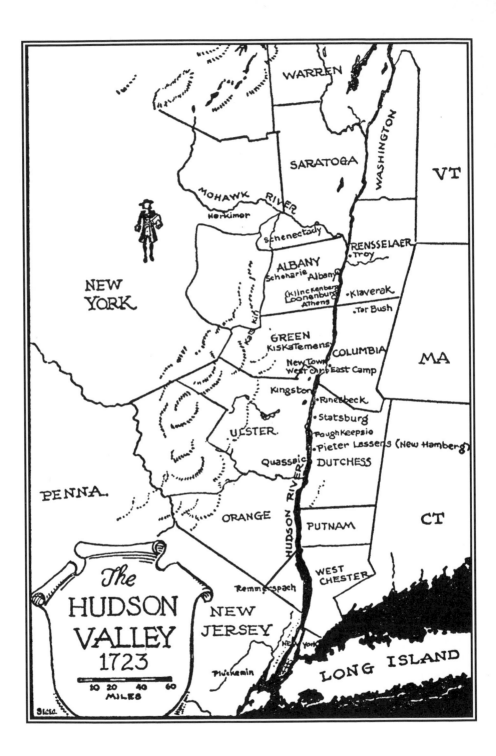

The
HUDSON
VALLEY
1723

10 20   40   60
MILES

WARREN

SARATOGA

WASHINGTON

VT

MOHAWK   RIVER
Herkimer

Schenectady

RENSSELAER
• Troy

ALBANY
Schoharie   Albany
(K)lncKenberg
Loonenburg   • Klaverak
Athens
• Tar Bush

GREEN
KisKaTemens

COLUMBIA

MA

NewTown
West Camp East Camp

Kingston
• Rinebeck
• Statsburg
• PoughKeepsie
• Pieter Lassens (New Hamberg)

ULSTER.

Quassaic   DUTCHESS

NEW
YORK

HUDSON RIVER

Kaaterskil

PENNA.

ORANGE

PUTNAM

CT

WEST
CHESTER

Remmerspach

NEW
JERSEY

New York

PlucKemin

LONG ISLAND

6

❧ 1 ❧

The Falckner Family

The three surviving sons of Pastor Daniel Falckner of Langenreinsdorf, just south of Crimmitschau, Saxony, didn't have to wonder about what they were going to do with their lives. They would all be ordained as Lutheran pastors, just as their father and grandfathers on both sides had done for six generations. It was part of the guild organization of 17th century Europe that sons almost always did what their fathers did.[1] If it was a family of pastors then the sons would come home after their theological studies at the university and Ordination to assist their father, or they might be called to a parish where the incumbent had died without children. If there was a young widow in a parish rectory the new incumbent was expected to marry her or alternately her daughter. The famous story about Johann Sebastian Bach's journey to Lübeck and his refusal to accept the position of Cantor at the Marienkirche because of the requirement to marry his predecessor's widow, was not unusual.

In the case of the Falckner family, the grandfather Christian is listed in an early 20th century parish history of Langenreinsdorf as the sixth pastor after the Reformation, 1635-1654, and Justus' father as the seventh after the Reformation, 1655-1674.[2] The same volume gives us these few words of description about the grandfather:

Christian Falckner was formerly pastor in Ziegra.
Only occasionally did he make note of the suffering
of his congregation in the Thirty Years War. Three
years before his death, on 5 November 1658, he obtained
his son as a substitute, the successor, Daniel Falckner, who
died here on 9 April 1674. Of his period in office little is
known.[3]

Daniel Falckner's three sons were Paul Christian, baptized February 2, 1662; Daniel Jr., born November 25, 1666; and Justus, born November 22, 1672. The parish register tells us that Justus was born about 10:00 AM and that he was baptized on November 24, the 25th Sunday after Trinity. His sponsors were Hans Gräfe; Maria, wife of Martin Drommers of Rudelswalde, and Paul Kretzschmar.[4] One would expect the daughter in the family, Maria Margaretha, born July, 1660, to have married a Lutheran pastor or widower. We know from a letter written by Daniel, Jr. that she was still alive in 1702, living in Altenburg,[5] and apparently known to August Herman Francke. The family had nine children altogether but the other five did not live until maturity: Martin (Feb, 10, 1658-June 14, 1666); Elisabeth (April 17, 1659-July 4, 1659); Christiane Barbara (May 28,1665-October 8, 1665)); Anna Katharina (January 18, 1669-January 23, 1672); and Susanne Lina (December 13, 1670-April 18, 1673).

While the sons inherited their father's profession, in the case of Daniel, Jr. and the youngest son, Justus, the field of service would be in America rather than in Saxony. The reason seems to be related to their move away from Langenreinsdorf following their father's death while they were still minors, their university studies, and the beginning of the movement in church history known as Pietism.

Pietism began in Germany as a turn away from the strict orthodoxy of the post-Reformation generations. It was nothing less than a revolution. It emphasized a personal appropriation of faith, study of the Scriptures, mystical experience, practical solutions to social problems, and public witness to the Christian faith. In its best forms it led to an increasing sense of social responsibility, a democratization of institutions, a remarkable hymnody, an ecumenical awareness, and an interest in missions outside of one's own country. In its worst forms it led to bizarre, at times even psychotic, episodes where subjectivity reigned, morals were narrowly defined, and emotionalism exploded.

The beginnings of Pietism are usually traced to Philip Jakob Spener (1635-1705), at first pastor in Frankfurt-am-Main, later court preacher to the Elector of Saxony in Leipzig and finally pastor of St. Nicholas Church in Berlin. In its later forms in America, its consequences led to the Great Awakenings and the revivals on the frontier. One strand of the origins of today's mega-church movement is to be found in Pietism. In Germany at the end of the 17th century it had led to the foundation of the University of Halle. Here taught the famous August Herman Francke (1663-1727).[6] Francke had experienced a vivid conversion in 1687 at the University of Leipzig. He organized a group for Bible study and devotions, demanding that theological students be "saved" and that they be concerned about the salvation of others. It was not enough to be able to argue over theological facts, it was right experience that counted.

All over Germany small home groups (collegia) were formed.[7] Sometimes they assisted peoples' devotions but sometimes they were divisive, demanding that everyone be "converted" according to their own model. When Francke ran afoul of the Leipzig authorities, he took refuge at the new University of Halle. Soon, in the neighboring town of Glaucha, he had established a charity school, an orphanage, a teacher training school, an infirmary, a printing house, and a medicine factory. The latter two brought revenue to the foundation and provided solutions to pressing needs. The first Bibles that were small enough to be held in one's hands were printed at Halle.

The older brothers, Paul Christian and Daniel, Jr., both studied at the University of Leipzig. Paul Christian matriculated in the summer of 1675, and Daniel, Jr. in the summer of 1688. Although there are no records of what they studied, we may assume that it was theology.[8] Justus matriculated at Halle on June 20, 1692, just as the new university was starting up its first classes.[9] We know little about his actual studies. He would have had Francke as a professor of Biblical languages and Christian Thomasius, a liberal freethinker, formerly of Leipzig, for philosophy. In itself these two professors tell us a great deal about Justus. From Francke he would have gained the zeal and warmth that showed Pietism at its best. From Thomasius he would have gained a progressive social orientation and emphasis on the use of his intellect. Both of these strengths would be put to the test when he arrived in Pennsylvania. No doubt he met the thirteen Swedish theological students who were registered there at the same time.[10] The next year Justus is found enrolled at Leipzig, apparently following the German tradition of studying at several schools.[11] In fact there was no one prescribed course of study for the Ministry. One studied Greek, Latin, Hebrew, dogmatics and exegesis and, after three to six years, applied for an examination before a Consistory.

Justus seems to have continued his studies, but was not ordained. This was not unusual since there were more candidates than available positions. We find him in Lübeck and then Rostock, where he was also probably studying. He seems to have made the acquaintance of the Superintendent (Bishop) of Schlesvig, Heinrich Mühlen, and then was in Holstein as a tutor and schoolteacher. Both of his paternal grandparents had died before he was born and his father had died when he was only two years old, so he could not return to Langenreinsdorf as his assistant.[12] It is probable that when his father died the family moved to the mother's home town of Lissen (Lössen), a town just south of Halle. There his maternal grandfather, Pastor Domini M[agister] Michaelis Möbius was both a local pastor in Lissen and Handorff and a dean [probst]. Perhaps Justus' interest in the pietistic revolution and the move away from his ancestral town had given him a wider vision of service.

❧ 2 ❧

The Frankfurt Land Company

The great Englishman, William Penn (1644-1718), not only invited members of his Society of Friends to settle in his personal proprietorship of Pennsylvania, but he had also traveled to Germany to invite religious dissidents to cross the Atlantic. He had already impressed a group of pietists in Frankfurt-am-Main in 1677, and several of them began a correspondence with Penn's agent in Rotterdam, Benjamin Furly. Just as Penn received his charter, (1681), a lawyer by the name of Francis (Franz) Daniel Pastorius came to Frankfurt and became involved in the plans. He went to Rotterdam and purchased 15,000 acres of land "on a navigable stream" near Philadelphia and agreed to enlist sufficient settlers. He found a group of Mennonite weavers in Crefeld, near the Dutch border, and by 1691 "Germantown," eight miles beyond Philadelphia, was organized. Naturally the word spread all over Germany, helped by a Latin treatise written by Pastorius.[13]

Daniel Falckner, Jr. had come under the influence of a group of radical pietists at Halle led by Johann Jacob Zimmermann, who had served as a Lutheran pastor, as a professor, and was currently working as a "corrector" for a printing establishment.[14] He was an accomplished scientist and mathematician, advocating the Copernican model of the universe. He had become convinced that the end of the world was near and that for the return of Christ, it was necessary to leave the depravity of Europe and go into the wilderness. His astronomical and mathematical calculations advised him that time was short before the Millennium would begin.

Making up a group with the symbolic number of forty, Zimmermann's followers called themselves Theosophists, i.e. those who would devote themselves to the knowledge of God.[15] They left Frankfurt and arrived in Rotterdam in 1693. There

Zimmermann died, but the group, including Daniel Falckner, a dissident Lutheran teacher named Heinrich Bernhard Köster, and the newly-elected leader, Magister Johannes Kelpius, pushed on to England and finally to Pennsylvania.[16] The leader's title is significant. "Magister" is the equivalent of today's doctorate and was awarded only for the highest attainments.

The choice of Kelpius was fortunate. He was the son of a Lutheran pastor in Denndorf, Transylvania (in present-day Romania), who had graduated from the University of Altdorf in 1689, an institution known for its staunch Lutheran orthodoxy. He was fluent in five languages. He carried on long theological correspondences and his humble manner endeared him to everyone. He was known as a visionary and psychic. He had musical and poetical ability, writing a number of hymns that were published at his death in 1708 and which were later sung by the Ephrata community in Pennsylvania. In fact it was the piety of Kelpius that attracted Conrad Beisel to America, not knowing that the Magister had already died. His famous "Seventh Day Baptist" community in Ephrata owed much of its inspiration to the community that Kelpius had established on the Wissahickon.[17]

❧ 3 ❧

The Hermits on the Wissahickon

It was Midsummer's Eve, June 23, 1694, when the pietistic community reached Philadelphia. They had received a tract of 175 acres on the hilly banks of the Wissahickon Creek, a tributary to the Schuylkill River. It wound up the hills to the ridge on which Germantown had been placed. The location was ideal for their purposes. Each hermit was to have his own small dwelling or cave and there was a common forty-foot square log "Tabernacle" where daily worship, open to the public, was held.[18] Following western monastic tradition, the brothers wore white habits. They planted small garden plots, developed herbal medicines, provided spiritual direction, cast horoscopes, set type,[19] did book binding, spent many hours in astronomical observations, developed a musical repertoire with what was one of the first pipe organs in America,[20] and provided a free school for young boys.

John Greenleaf Whittier's 1872 poem, "The Pennsylvania Pilgrim," which is mainly an idealized picture of Pastorius, contains these rather accurate lines about Kelpius:

…Or painful Kelpius from his hermit den
By Wissahickon, maddest of good men,
Dreamed o'er the Chiliast dreams of Petersen.

Deep in the woods where the small river slid
Snake-like in shade, the Helmstedt Mystic hid
Weird as a wizard, over arts forbid.

Reading the books of Daniel and of John,
And Behmen's[21] Morning redness through the Stone
Of Wisdom, vouchsafed to his eyes alone,

Whereby he read what man ne'er read before

And saw the visions man shall see no more,
Till the great angel, striding sea and shore,

Shall bid all flesh await, on land or ships,
The warning trump of the Apocalypse
Shattering the heavens before the dread eclipse.[22]

Yet the hoped-for return of Christ did not materialize and some began to drift away. The mystical number of forty was no longer fulfilled. Heinrich Köster got into trouble with both the Quakers and the inhabitants of Germantown after he had organized Lutheran services in both Germantown and Philadelphia. At one point he even seems to have baptized some Quakers in the Delaware River and in general sided with the dissenting Quaker and soon-to-be Anglican priest, George Keith.[23] Pastorius was so upset that he quit his position as representative of the Frankfurt Land Company and Köster returned to Germany.

In this time of confusion Daniel Falckner was selected to go to Germany and confer with the backers of the Frankfurt Land Company and with Francke in Halle. His conversations with Francke, in question and answer form, were published first in Germany in 1700 and then in 1702 an abstract came out entitled, *Curious Account of Pennsylvania in North America which at solicitation of good friends regarding 103 questions submitted, and at his departure from Germany to above Country, Anno 1700, are answered and Now, Anno 1702, are given in print by Daniel Falckner, Professor, Citizen and pilgrim there.*[24] No doubt this report stimulated wide interest in Germany about the Pennsylvania colony. No English translation of these works was made at the time but it was later translated and published by the Pennsylvania German Society[25].

The reports that Falckner gave to Benjamin Furly in Rotterdam, and to the other members of the Frankfurt Land Company at Amsterdam, Lübeck and Frankfurt led to the official dismissal of Pastorius. A power of attorney was written out to authorize Daniel and Justus Falckner, along with Johann Jauert and Magister Johannes Kelpius, to take charge of the company's business in Pennsylvania. We have no idea how Daniel talked his younger brother into returning with him to Pennsylvania, but Justus was obviously not satisfied with his life in Germany at the time. He was 27 years old, unmarried and had not been ordained.

Justus thus arrived with his brother in August, 1700, ready to reform the governance of Germantown in this "western land" [Abend-land, referring to the direction in which the sun sets].[26] The city of Philadelphia then had about 2,700 inhabitants, and the borough of Germantown about three hundred people living along Germantown Pike. Justus was the first student from Halle to serve in North America and the precursor of Johann Martin Bolzius in Georgia (1734), Henry Melchior Muhlenberg (1742) in the middle colonies, as well as countless others.

By December of 1700 Daniel Falckner was chosen bailiff and Justus as a burgess of Germantown. Yet politics was not Justus' calling. He found himself drawn to Kelpius on the Wissahickon and was shocked by the wide diversity of religious opinions that thrived in Pennsylvania. As he lived alone in his hermitage, studying and praying with the other theosophists, he remembered that he had promised to report on conditions to the Superintendent (Bishop) of Schlesvig, Henrich Mühlen. His letter, written in August, 1701, and translated by Julius Sachse in 1903 gives us a good idea of his reactions.[27]

> ...I have gone more among the people, and subsequently have resolved to give up the solitude I have thus far maintained, and according to my humble powers, to strive at least with good intention publicly to assist in doing and effecting good in this spiritual and corporeal wilderness. So far as I am able to draw conclusions concerning the conditions of churches in these parts...it is still pretty bad. The Aborigines or Indians, from lack of sufficient good instruction, remain in their blindness and barbarity, and moreover are angered at the bad living of the Christians,

especially at the system of trading which is driven with them, and they learn only vices which they did not have formerly, such as drunkenness, stealing, etc. The local Christian minority however is divided into almost innumerable sects, which pre-eminently may be called sects and hordes, as Quakers, Anabaptists, Naturalists, Rationalists, Independents, Sabbatarians, and many others, especially secret insinuating sects...The Quakers are the most numerous, because the Governor favors this sect...It would easily make a whole treatise were I only to set forth how they, by transgressing their own principles, show in plain daylight the kind of spirit that moves them, when they virtually scoff at the foundation of such principles, and become Ishmaels of all well regulated church-institutions.

The Protestant Church however, is here divided into three confessions and nations...and are either of the Evangelical Lutheran, or of the Presbyterian, or of the Calvinistic Church...and so there are here an English Protestant Church and a Swedish Protestant Lutheran Church; and also persons of the German nation of the Evangelical Lutheran and Reformed churches...

The Swedes have two church congregations: one at Philadelphia, the capital of this country, and another several miles therefrom on a river called Christina [Wilmington, Delaware]. They have also two devout, learned and conscientious preachers, among whom I know *in specie* the Reverend Magister Rudman. He, with his colleagues, endeavors to instill the true fear and knowledge of God into his hearers, who previously, from a lack of good instruction and church discipline, had become rather unruly. The outward worship of God is held in the Swedish language, and partly according to the Swedish liturgy, so far as church ceremonies are concerned.

The Germans, however, I have spoken of not without cause as merely several Evangelical Lutheran Germans, and not the German Evangelical Lutheran Church: those who are destitute of altar and priest forsooth roam about in this desert...a deplorable condition indeed. Moreover there is here a large number of Germans who, however, have partly crawled in among the different sects who use the English tongue. A number are Quakers and Anabaptists; a portion are Free-Thinkers and assimilate with no one. They also allow their children to grow up in the same manner.

In short there are Germans here, and perhaps the majority, who despise God's Word and all outward good order; who blaspheme the Sacraments, and frightfully and publicly give scandal (for the spirit of errors and sects has here erected for itself an asylum...).

Now I recommend to Your Magnificence, as an intelligent German Evangelical theologian...on account of the wretched condition of the German Evangelical communities, some establishment of an evangelical church assembly could be made in America, since the Germans are now increasing rapidly...

Both myself and my brother, who is sojourning here, keep ourselves to the Swedish church, although we understand little or nothing of the language...Above all one of the Swedish pastors, Magister Rudman, has offered, regardless of the difficulty, to assume the German dialect. For nothing less than the love of God's honor he has offered to go to this trouble now and then to deliver a German address in the Swedish church, until the Germans can have a church of their own, together with the necessary establishment. Accordingly the Germans who still love the evangelical truth, and a proper outward church order, much prefer to attend the Swedish churches here until they can also have their divine worship in their own language as a people...The means are hereby offered in a measure to spread the Gospel truth in these wilds, whereby many of their brethren and fellow-countrymen may be brought from wrong to right, from darkness to light, and from the whirlpool of sectaries to the peace and quiet of the true Church...

I will here take occasion to mention that many others besides myself, who know the ways of this land, maintain that music would contribute much towards a good Christian service...Instrumental music is especially serviceable here. Thus a well-sounding organ would perhaps prove of great profit...as the melancholy saturnine stingy Quaker spirit has abolished all such music. It would be a novelty here, and tend to attract many of the young people away from the Quakers and sects to attend services where such music was found, even against the wishes of their parents. This would afford a good opportunity to show them the truth and their error…If such an organ-instrument were placed in the Swedish church (for the Germans as yet have no church and the Swedish church is of high build and resonant structure) it would prove a great service to this church…And it may be assumed that even a small organ-instrument and music in this place would be acceptable to God, and prove more useful than many hundreds in Europe, where there is already a superfluity of such things; and the more common they are, the more they are misused.

    If now your Magnificence were kindly to intercede with his Serene Highness and Her Highness his Consort, …and present them the benefit to be hoped for, I doubt not that something could be effected…

Apparently nothing came of his plea either for the beginning of a German mission to America or for a pipe organ for Gloria Dei, Old Swedes Church in Philadelphia. At the time of his writing, no German principality was able to look beyond its borders to a mission field abroad. It was not until 1705 that Fredrik IV of Denmark would send Bartolomeus Ziegenbalg and Heinrich Plütschau to minister to the Danish colony in Tranqebar, India. But the vision, which Justus had for a German mission patterned on that of the Church of Sweden, as renewed in 1697, shows his concern for his countrymen. He is on the way to his Ordination, some two years later.

He seems to have left the Hermits and settled in German-town, since in 1702 Daniel Falckner writes to Francke, saying that Justus is busy helping him in the real estate business and thus cannot be hired as a needed schoolteacher.[28]

❧ 4 ❧

Andreas Rudman

Andreas Rudman was born in 1668 in Gävle, Sweden. He completed his theological studies at Uppsala University and was ordained in 1696. He was chosen by Archbishop Svebelius and Dean Jesper Svedberg to lead the delegation of pastors to renew the work of the Church of Sweden in the Delaware Valley. This was a unique moment in the history of world missions. It is from this date that world missions should be dated in the history of Protestant missiology. For in this case the pastors were not "following the flag" and providing chaplaincy services to an expatriate community. The provision of pastors to America was simply the result of a need and request from Americans for pastoral leadership.[29]

The Church of Sweden Mission to America had begun in 1640, just two years after the establishment of the colony at Ft. Christina in Wilmington, Delaware. It was then that the first pastor, Torkil Reorus[30] came and afterwards a series of five other priests served the colony. The most famous of them, Johan Campanius, who served 1643-1648, translated Luther's *Small Catechism* into the language of the local Indians. This was the first book printed in the Algonquin language. When the colony was lost to the Dutch in 1655 the only priest who remained was Lars Lock. He stayed and served until his death in 1688. By the terms of the surrender, the Swedes were allowed one priest of the Augsburg Confession for their religious needs.[31]

Following the English conquest, the congregation that remained at Tinicum Island and that which had begun to worship at Wicaco/Philadelphia called Jacob Fabritius as pastor in 1677. He was a Silesian who had served the Dutch Lutherans in New York and Albany. When he died in 1696 there were no Lutheran pastors in the Delaware Valley. But the congregations had written to Sweden already in 1693 and asked that the mission be renewed with two new priests, one for the upper congregation at Philadelphia/Wicaco and one for the southern congregation at Wilmington/Tranhuk. King Carl XI favorably received the letter, and an appended census of all the Swedish families living in the Delaware Valley along with the Americans' promise of monetary support. He asked the aged Archbishop of Uppsala and the dynamic Jesper Svedberg, Dean of Uppsala Cathedral and professor of homiletics at the university, to select the candidates.[32]

Rudman was the first to be selected. He had achieved the advanced degree of "Magister." He was the only one of the first three Swedish priests in the renewed mission who had such a degree. He was given the title"Primarius" and a larger travel allowance than the other two priests who accompanied him. His title is significant. It recalls the title given to the pastor of the Great Church of St. Nicholas in Stockholm (Pastor Primarius) who, while not being a bishop, had episcopal duties as directed by the monarch. While this church is today the Cathedral of the Stockholm Diocese, before 1942 it served as a sort of pro-cathedral adjacent to the Royal Palace.

In an age when Church and State were intimately connected, the King's word had ecclesiastical validity. In fact, according to the Church Ordinance of 1686, the King named the bishops of the regular sees after an ecclesiastical ballot among the priests was presented to him. The King was not bound to take the person with the greatest number of votes but the one he considered most "suitable."[33] Since the Middle Ages monarchs had named bishops, and the habit continued in Lutheran Sweden, without the necessity of consulting with the Papacy. A candidate chosen to be a bishop was then consecrated with an appropriate liturgical ceremony, although superintendents did not have a liturgical consecration. The King not only named bishops but had the prerogative of naming the Senior Pastors for a number of diocesan parishes, the so-called, "regal parishes." In the Baltic countries, which were then under Swedish rule, the King named almost all of the priests,[34] although they still had to be ordained by a bishop or superintendent.

This was particularly the case with King Carl XI, the most autocratic of the monarchs of seventeenth century Sweden.[35] In the age of Louis XIV, he didn't have to be reminded of the golden key that he had been given at his coronation, along with an orb and scepter, as a sign of his Petrine vocation. His family tree was traced back to Noah and he was considered to have inherited all of the virtues of the Old Testament kings.[36] He was responsible to God for the well being of the faith of the people and it was he who paid for the priests to travel to America. He was, however, required to follow the Scriptures and the laws. Yet it was the naming that was considered vital to the function of bishop and not the liturgical reception of such an office.

In addition, Bishop Svedberg in the unpublished manuscripts that are collected in *Svecia Nova seu America Illuminata* tells us that Rudman had been given special permission by Archbishop Svebelius to ordain if it were necessary.[37] This seems to have happened before their departure in 1696. Indeed the famous Dean, Israel Acrelius (1714-1800), who was pastor at Wilmington and after returning to Sweden wrote a history of the colony, states that Rudman became a Superintendent already when he left Gloria Dei Church in July, 1702.[38]

In the 1720's when Falckner's ordination was cited by Anglicans as an example of a presbyterial ordination, the official answer from the Church of Sweden was that Rudman had been appointed as a Suffragan or Vice-Bishop by the Archbishop.[39] The additional paper documentation from the King was not mentioned and by implication should be seen as a confirmation of Rudman's functioning in an episcopal manner.

Another example of a Swedish priest who was named as a bishop but not yet consecrated and still was given the right to ordain is A. O. Rhyzelius, who had been named Bishop of Linköping on April 20, 1743, while the incumbent was still alive. He ordained in the nearby Cathedral of Skara on August 25, 1743, because of the death of their bishop.[40]

Further confirmation of Rudman's stature can be seen in that when the three new priests arrived in June of 1697, Rudman was given his choice of parishes and he chose the Church at Wicaco, Philadelphia, the capital of the colony.

As pastor of the Church in Philadelphia, he oversaw between 1698 and 1700, the construction of the brick building that still stands in South Philadelphia, giving it the unique name of "Gloria Dei," the Church of God's Glory.

Rudman was also an amateur musician and poet. He wrote two small pamphlets that contained eight hymns that were published in 1700. They are the first hymnals to be published in this country, and the first Swedish imprints in the Americas.

When William Penn returned to his colony in 1699 for his last visit, Rudman extracted a grant from him of 10,000 acres on the Manatawny Creek (near Douglassville, Pa.) in compensation for the preemption of so much land from the Swedes in the Philadelphia area. This 1701 grant was adjacent to Falckner's Swamp, named for Daniel and under his direction, where the Frankfurt Land Company had established another German settlement, near present day Gilbertsville. The name "swamp" was actually an anglicization of the German word for meadow and the German congregations there known as New Hanover Lutheran Church and Falckner's Swamp Reformed Church consider themselves the oldest German congregations of their denominations in the United States. The Lutheran congregation lists Daniel Falckner as its first pastor in 1700, although reliable evidence for the formal organization of the congregation is available only with the arrival of Anthony Jacob Henkel (1668-1728) in 1717.[41]

With the completion of Gloria Dei church and in failing health, Rudman requested to return to Sweden. But letters from the Dutch Lutheran congregation in the province of New York changed his course. The congregation dated back to 1649 but was in danger of total collapse. A letter written on September 29, 1701, said simply:

Honorable and learned Minister and Friend.

Sir, these letters per mail have honored us to the highest, and we are inclined to your dignity, in which is found your Lordship's good fondness with the community over here, for which we are grateful to you to the highest. And wishing that we may have the honor to speak with your Reverence, we would be pleased to hear the godly Trumpet from the minister's mouth; it will not happen that we will be absent then. And we will pray that God the Lord will give your Reverence his inner thoughts to protect his Flock. With this we entrust your Reverence in the protection of the Highest and will remain, my Lord, your Reverence's pre-obliged and affectionate Friends and Servants.

> By order of the Elders
> And Church masters
> D. V. Burgh [42]

When Andreas Sandel came to replace him in 1702, Rudman felt impelled to answer the requests from the Dutch Lutherans of New York City and Albany county to revive their congregations.

The Germans in Germantown wrote a poem to him expressing their thanksgiving when it became known that he was leaving. The poem is signed by Daniel Falckner, Justus Falckner and Daniel Liedke, and since only Justus is known to have had poetic ability we can probably say that he is the author:

Rudman, shepherd to the poor Swedes
Came to this country at a fitting time.
When error threatened to thwart the
Wakeful teaching of Luther,
You taught anew.
Every work gives praise to its master
And to the master comes great reward.
Rudman detests empty spirits and
Preaches the Christianity of God's Son.
His life, teachings and vocation focus
On praising God, rather than praising self.[43]

Rudman's own feelings on the matter are expressed in a letter to the Archbishop and Consistory at Uppsala written on June 16, 1702:

...And it happens that I have promised [to assist] the Dutch Lutheran Church in New York, who have had no teacher [pastor] now for 12 years, but now after many requests to Amsterdam, expect to get some help. For when I saw myself as not specially wanting to do this over the winter, they were perplexed because of the many various years and times I had visited and helped them. I thought that I could not in any way better use my time than to come to the aid of such poor, scattered sheep, and to put on its feet the [Dutch] Congregation, which almost in a similar way is as this one was at first. If I am able to do this, I would count myself as the most fortunate [of men] who has had the grace to take care of four congregations in this heathen country, namely our Swedish, the High German, for whom at various times I preached and administered the Sacraments in our own church and in German Town (their own city located 6 miles from Philadelphia), the English Church for a little while, and now the Dutch.[44]

He preached his final sermon at Philadelphia on July 19, 1702, and left for New York City. Things were indeed grim there. The old building on Broadway at Rector Street, which dated from 1676, was in poor condition and there had been no regular pastor since the death of Bernhardus Arnzius eleven years earlier. To make matters worse, Rudman soon became ill from yellow fever and his son died from the same disease. Yet he managed to stabilize the congregations and begin the official record book that is still in existence. And most importantly he provided for a successor.

This letter written to Justus Falckner in Latin on September 21, 1703, gives his thoughts:

...But only listen, I beg you: for I am going to give you some unexpected news, for you to seriously and prayerfully ponder. I have decided to leave this province, to dispose of my affairs in Pennsylvania for some time, and to revisit Sweden. What! You ask; are you going to desert your flock? Wherefore, as I look around, no one has occurred to me as a more suitable person to whom I can safely commit my sheep than yourself. Only weigh the following reasons:

(1) The call will be plainly divine. Samuel, when called of God, thought, "Shall I ask Eli" whence is this? Whence can it be, unless God has imitated the voice of Eli! So, be assured,

(2) God is calling you through me. So far as I have heard from the people, all agree, and that too, with great delight.

(3) In Europe, you could have obtained greater and more lucrative churches; but I know that you have been averse to this on account of the abandoned life of the courtiers and others. Here matters are very different; guileless scattered sheep, few, docile, obedient, thirsty and famished.

(4) You seem to have been called from the womb. Will you bury your talent with a good conscience?

(5) You have dignified me with the name of "Father." Receive therefore the exhortation of a father. If I can persuade the Ministerium, you will be initiated (*sacre ordini*) into the ministry by our Swedish ministers.

If you decline, I will be compelled to leave my sheep without a successor, and this will be hard and difficult.[45]

Justus still seemed to be unsure so that Rudman had to write to him again on October 4, 1703.

Episcopal authority for consecrating churches, ordaining, etc. has been granted to me unreservedly by the [Arch] bishop, especially with reference to a contingency such as this. This was done previously in Pennsylvania among the Swedes by Rev. Laurentius Lock who ordained Avelius, there, etc. Beside you know that in Holland, Lutherans have no bishop and are, therefore, inducted into the ministry by the vote of the presbyters. You should have no doubt whatever, therefore, concerning the fact of which I assure you, that, if you prefer to be the subject of his protection and promotion, the Bishop of Sweden will transmit his confirmation.[46]

Rudman was depending on hearsay for his reference to Avelius, who is really Abelius Zetskoorn. Zetskoorn was a Dutch Lutheran schoolmaster who worked for some time at New Castle, and even preached once at the old church at Tinicum, but who was opposed by Lars Lock. He returned unordained to New Amsterdam since Lock did not want to share any part of the work with him. There is no record of him administering any sacramental functions, although he is listed as preaching in New York City. On the subject of there being no bishops in the Lutheran Church of the Netherlands, Rudman was of course correct.

It is instructive that the subject of proper order figures so prominently in the correspondence. Justus was not about to be ordained by any available priest. He wanted the ordination to be a recognized act of the Church that would be acceptable to the governmental authorities in New York, the Amsterdam Consistory and his clerical colleagues in the Anglican Church. Interestingly he shows no enthusiasm for traveling to Manhattan for a trial sermon before the ordination.

Neither Erik Björk, who served in Wilmington and wrote extensively and critically about a number of things, nor Andreas Sandel, who was well known in Sweden, and had been a classmate of Rudman's, had any objections to the proposed Ordination. Rudman probably reported the proposal to the King and to Jesper Svedberg who had just been appointed Bishop of Skara. King Carl XI had died soon after the three priests left for America, and a new King, Carl XII, one of the most brilliant military tacticians to hold power in Europe, was in Poland defending Sweden's interests. In those days a letter addressed to a King in Stockholm and then relayed on to a foreign battlefield might take eight months to arrive. Thus it was not until January 22, 1704, that the King wrote to Rudman and regularly appointed him as his Superintendent (Bishop) in America. The text of his appointment as the first episcopal church official in the original Thirteen Colonies reads as follows:

> WE CARL by the Grace of God, King of Sweden, the Goths, and the Wends, Grand Duke of Finland,....make known that since we have graciously had concern for the Swedish colonists out in New Sweden or Pennsylvania in America, we think fit to appoint a Superintendent there, who would rule over the propagation of the pure Evangelical [Lutheran] teaching and good order and take care of all necessary things, and as it has been reported to us about his untiring diligence and watchfulness for us and the beloved Worthy and Learned Magister Andreas Rudman has supervised divine services at the named congregations for many years;...For we have herewith and in the power of this Our public letter, graciously willed to call and ordain him, Magister Andreas Rudman, to be our Superintendent and have oversight over church affairs, at the named Swedish Congregations in America, commanding all to whom this applies, and who are indebted to us, that they may show him the honor and obedience which belongs to this same Office....Given at Heilsberg, Prussia on the 22nd January 1704.[47]

It is clear from the 1686 Church Ordinance of the Church of Sweden that the Office of Bishop and that of Superintendent were identical.[48] The Superintendents were appointed to diocesan areas that had become too large to administer or to areas that were not yet ready for full diocesan organization with a Cathedral Chapter/ Consistory. They ordained, made episcopal visitations, preached and watched over the work of the Church. Thus there were at this time Superintendents in Gothenburg, Karlstad, Kalmar, Narva, Viborg and Riga, to mention just a few.[49]

The Archbishop of Uppsala, Eric Benzelius, also approved of Rudman's appointment as can be seen from a pastoral letter to the Swedish Congregations in America, dated about six weeks after the King's on the 2nd of March, 1704.

...Therefore, now at this time, our reigning monarch, King Carl XII has graciously found it good to ordain M. Andreas Rudman to be Superintendent there, who for long time there in those places has given proof of diligent establishment and improvement of congregations. Accordingly he may voluntarily take care not only of the advancement of the Evangelical [Lutheran] Teaching, but also assist, as conscience allows, other church people who can appear, and should be promptly answered...[50]

It is interesting that the Archbishop specifically sees the responsibility of a Superintendent as multiethnic and ecumenical. He is to serve the Swedish congregations but also other "church people" who would include the German and Dutch Lutherans and the Anglicans.

By late 1703, Justus seemed open to accept the call and the ordination. The Church Council in New York on October 27, 1703, wrote to him to come for a trial sermon. Three days later they sent their official call. Since the trial sermon was not an absolute necessity, Rudman made preparations to leave New York and arrange the ordination at Gloria Dei in Philadelphia.

He had to confer with Erik Björk from Holy Trinity in Wilmington and his successor at Gloria Dei, Andreas Sandel. Jonas Aurén had come along with the other two priests as a cartographer and had founded a congregation (St. Mary's) in North East, Maryland, in addition to visiting the Indians on the Susquehanna frontier. At this time, he had begun to be a Sabbatarian and in his final sermon Rudman had warned the congregation in Philadelphia about Aurén's heretical position.[51] The other Swedish priest in the Delaware Valley, Lars Tolstadius, had arrived without a commission from the King. Rudman had taken him to New York in May, 1702, hoping to interest him in either New York or Albany. The New York City Congregation preferred Rudman or was willing to wait even longer for the Amsterdam Consistory to send them a candidate. Tolstadius was not interested in Albany and thus returned with Rudman to the Delaware Valley where he completed the organization of a rival congregation in Swedesboro, New Jersey

(1702)[52]. Neither Aurén nor Tolstadius would be invited to participate in Falckner's Ordination. By November 19, 1703, Erik Björk would write to Falckner to further encourage him and express his approval:

> ...You sought a hiding-place; but He from whom no one can hide is now seeking to call you hence. Come forth then to the light and profit of the public. For nothing will be more pleasing to God, than for you to devote your life to the common good, particularly of souls...We have been born not for ourselves, but for others, especially for God and his Church, and for which your services are needed here, more than they could have been elsewhere in your native land, you have been brought hither without thought or intention on your part.[53]

Justus must have been persuaded since the time and place were soon arranged.

❧ 5 ❧

The Ordination, November 24, 1703

A ndreas Sandel, the pastor of Gloria Dei at Philadelphia from
1702-1719 gives us the facts quite simply in his parish record
book for the year 1703:

> Since Magister Rudman's health was not good in New York,
> he called a German student Mr. Justus Falckner to take his
> place. Then we 3 priests, Mr. Rudman, Mr. Björk, and I
> ordained him as a priest in Wicaco in the presence of the
> congregation.[54]

It was a Wednesday and the liturgy probably took place in
the forenoon because of the lack of adequate lighting in the new
church building. Falckner had celebrated his 31st birthday just two
days earlier. It was also the exact anniversary of his Baptism in
Langenreinsdorf. We have a good idea of what Gloria Dei Church
looked like since after its dedication (July 2, 1700) Andreas Rudman
wrote a letter on November 20, 1700, providing a description:

> The church is 60 feet long, 30 feet wide, and 20 feet high.
> The roof is made of cedar shingles, 18,000 of them. There
> are six windows, three on each side, 12 feet high. The whole
> interior is covered with plaster, although the ceiling was first
> secured with lathes. On each side the pews are arranged in
> two quarters, and in addition there is a lengthwise pew under
> the windows, with an aisle between this and the quarters.
> The entire chancel stands three steps higher than the church
> floor, so that the chancel rail and the pews are of the same
> height, and the altar rail as well.
>
> The altar, like the church, is made of brick. As its form, in
> time, will show, the tower is joined to the church, though
> still unfinished, approximately 26 or 28 feet high. In this is
> our entrance. Above there is a room for church articles, and

Gloria Dei Church, Wicaco (Philadelphia) as it appears today

over this a room for the church library. A bell room is to go over this, and also a spire, so that it may reach 80 or 100 feet in all...In the beginning we thought the church would be too large, but we need all the space now, and a little adjoining room, besides, which is intended for an organ loft and organ.[55]

A few more details are added from a description by Andreas Sandel when he arrived in 1702.

[It] is a very fine church, with six large windows, brick walls, pews made of cedar, and a pulpit of walnut. In the summer we expect to build a sacristy and porch.[56]

Today Gloria Dei stands in the Southwark neighborhood of Philadelphia near the Delaware River as the oldest church in Pennsylvania. The porches were finally added in 1704 and the tower was probably not complete by the time of Falckner's Ordination. A major renovation in 1846 added side balconies, a window in the apse, a central pulpit, and later a new system of pews. Thus while the exterior is remarkably unchanged, the interior provides no original furnishings, except for the two carved wooden cherubim heads that may date back to the original building on Tinicum Island in 1646.

It is unlikely that there was an organ at this date. The job of bell-ringer, *klockare*, often meant that the person was a cantor, teacher, clerk or organist but not necessarily. The 1686 Church Ordinance only prescribed that the person should be literate. Thus when the minutes state that a *klockare* (clerk, cantor, assistant) by the name of Sven Kåhlsberg was chosen by the parish meeting in May, 1702, it does not mean that there was an instrument to play.[57] Indeed we know that Gloria Dei did not have a pipe organ as late as 1714 since on the 24th of November of that year Bishop Svedberg wrote back to them saying that he could send them neither bells nor an organ because of the war conditions.[58] However we may conjecture that some sort of instrument was used since we know that Rudman had brought a *spinet* with him in 1697 and the Wissahickon brothers seem to have had the first portable organ in the area. They would have been present, and Julius Sachse goes so far as to suggest that they also brought along other instruments to accompany the service such as a viol, oboes and kettledrums.[59]

In any case it was a musical occasion. Both the ordinand and the presiding officiant, Rudman were musical and had written hymns for public worship. Yet the method of accompaniment was not that of later centuries. A pipe organ was used for a prelude and postlude, considered as a part of the liturgy and as such listened to by the people in the pews. The organ announced the hymns and provided interludes but was not used during the actual singing of verses, which were rendered a cappella and often in alternation between the women's and men's sides of the congregation.[60] Members of the congregation owned their own hymnals if they were literate and memorized the hymns if they were not. Since the King had sent along 100 hymnals in 1697, presumably half of these would have ended up at Gloria Dei. They arrived unbound and Magister Kelpius was paid to do the bindings. In addition, the two small hymnals that Rudman had written and published in Philadelphia in 1700 were available.[61]

The altar would have been dressed with a fair linen and an antependium in either red, silver, black, or gold. The colors were not associated with the church year. Candlesticks were placed on the altar for light, the priest's book would have rested on a small pillow. Since the altar painting by Gustavus Hesselius was not yet in place there may have been a crucifix on the altar. The fact that the church contained an altar was unusual for British America. During the English Reformation all of the medieval stone altars had been removed and replaced by wooden tables. Thus the altars in the two Swedish churches were the only ones in the English-speaking colonies at the time, with the exception of those in the Roman Catholic churches in Maryland.

The priests who officiated no doubt wore albs. Since this was the standard liturgical vesture in Sweden, the priests probably brought along their own. In 1697 the Gloria Dei church books record the purchase of three yards of "red broadcloth" for a chasuble. At this time black and red were the preferred colors for such a vestment.[62] As the Officiant, Rudman would have worn this for the Ordination and then given it to Sandel to use for the Eucharist, since chasubles have an unbroken tradition of usage in Sweden. Stoles were not in use at the time; neither were amices or cinctures. In any case, such vestments were the property of the congregation, and were not given to ordinands.[63] Justus would have had no use for such vestments among the Reformed-influenced Lutherans of New York.

Thus the congregation that would have gathered at the ringing of the church bell would primarily be the Swedes, the Wissahickon brothers, and their fellow countrymen from Germantown. Certainly Justus' brother Daniel, Jr,. was there although it seems as if he had not been ordained yet. The very successful rector of the Anglican Christ Church, Evan Evans, was most likely present. In fact when the Dutch congregation wrote suggesting a trial sermon, they recommended that Rev. Evans be involved.[64] During a musical presentation the three vested priests entered led by Rudman carrying a veiled chalice and his liturgical books. After the priests would have come the candidate, dressed either in his black student frockcoat or his Wissahickon brotherhood alb, and then the Church Council: Caspar Fisk, Michael Laican, Anders Långåker, John Scute, John Stille and Matts Keen.[65] The *klockare* had probably taken his place after the ringing of the bells. The language of the Ordination itself was probably Latin, since we know that Rudman and Falckner corresponded in Latin and it was an easy matter to translate the Swedish Order of 1571/1686 into Latin. Yet it is also possible that Rudman asked the questions and allowed Falckner to say the oath in German. The hymns would have been mostly in Swedish as would have been the Eucharist that followed.

The Liturgy began with a hymn and a short Exhortation by Rudman as the Ordinarius in which he would have instructed the congregation about the Institution of the Preaching Office, the call of a priest, and the Office itself. After this everyone would kneel while the "*Veni Sancte Spiritus, reple tuorum corda fidelium*" was sung. This probably meant the three Swedish priests who had it memorized and the Wissahickon hermits. Then followed two collects: [66]

Almighty and everlasting God; the Father of Our Lord Jesus Christ, who himself has commanded us that we should pray for laborers in the harvest, that is for faithful preachers, we pray that in your unsearchable mercy you would indeed send us right-minded teachers, and give your holy and health-giving Word into their hearts and mouths, so that without all error, they may teach purely, and faithfully witness to all your commands, so that we, being instructed and admonished by your holy Word, may do that which is pleasing to you and necessary for us.

Grant us, O Lord, your Holy Spirit and wisdom, that your Word may always remain among us, grow and bear fruit, that your servants may preach the Word with the freedom that belongs to it, so that the Holy Christian Church may be edified and serve you in a steadfast faith, and remain forever in your knowledge. Through Jesus Christ, our Lord. Amen.

Following this, the candidate was asked to come forward and the congregation and office to which he was called was announced. He had been seated in a front pew since there were no chairs in the chancel. The announcement was probably done by Andreas Sandel as the *pastor loci*. Falckner then knelt as Rudman read:

Since you, Justus Falckner, are called to this service, which is the Office of a Priest, so now listen and give heed to these words which the Apostle of Jesus Christ, Saint Paul, has written about the same service and Office.

Then followed the reading of 1 Timothy 3:1-7; Titus 1: 7-9, and Acts 20: 28-31 (the 1541 Gustaf Vasa Bible used the translation of "bishops" for *episcopos* in verse 28).

Then Rudman continued with an Admonition leading up to the vows:

Herein one hears that of those who are called to be the church's shepherds [*kyrkoherdar*] and preachers, there is commanded a watch and guardianship, not over unreasonable things such as sheep and animals, but over the congregation of the living God, which He has redeemed with his own blood, that we should rule and feed her with the pure Word of God, and dutifully watch over [her], that wolves, that is false teachers, may not get in and do harm. Therefore He calls it a good and heartfelt work. We are also commanded in our personal life to exhibit a disciplined and honest life, and to keep our household, wife, children and servants, honest and Christian.

Then came the five-fold vows to which the candidate was instructed to answer "Yes" in a clear voice.

1. Will you now, in the name of God, the Holy Trinity, take up this service and Office of Priest?

2. Will you strive to rightly use it with dignity, to the glory of God and the good of his Church?

3. Will you always abide steadfastly in the pure word of God and flee from all false and heretical teachings?

4. Will you also regulate your own life so that you show forth a good example personally, giving no offence?

5. Wiil you always seek the general peace of the country, and promote loyalty and obedience to the proper authorities, as much as possible?

After the last question, and its response Falckner would have added:

I will do all of this gladly with God's grace and help.

Then followed the Oath, which the candidate read with his right hand placed on the Bible. It is unlikely that the long Oath of 1686 was used,[67] but a shorter form of it, like this, was possible:

I, Justus Falckner, who now am called and accepted to the Holy Office of Priest promise and swear before God and his Holy Gospel, that in its exercise, neither secretly to myself, nor publicly for my listeners will I disseminate and preach any other teaching, than that which God the Holy Spirit has himself dictated and extensively taught in the Holy Bible, but summarized in our Confession of Faith, and received Symbols, the Apostolic, as well as the Nicene and the Athanasian, as well as in the unaltered Augsburg Confession…

I will also rightly use and distribute the blessed Sacraments, and diligently conduct catechetical lessons with my listeners according to their understanding…I will also daily and honestly improve myself in God's Word and strengthen myself in the knowledge of the Articles of Faith, together with my other necessary studies, always seeking progress, and in no way neglecting them or putting them away.

I will also through God's Grace, correctly distribute [utdela] the Word of Truth, and exercise my Office in an orderly way, so as to show a godly, talented and sober life, fleeing all frivolous company, and superfluousness in food, drink and clothing, at the same time holding myself apart from all derisive and filthy talk, provoking acts, and impolite gestures, that in everything by word and deeds, I may present myself as a right-thinking Teacher and may thus provide others with a good example. I will also strive to hold among my listeners a correct and appropriate Church Discipline …exhorting them to the practice of godliness, the general peace of the country, honest living and company, together with internal unity and love, toward each other…

I will not involve myself in worldly, and to my Office improper, matters, or concern myself with such things, which are not fitting for a Priest and Teacher. I will beware of greed and filthy covetousness; and when I have been placed in a congregation, I will not demand more of my listeners, than is my right…

I will especially not oppress and bother the poor because of their conditions and abilities, even less those who have been wronged by the authorities, or hinder and refuse them the Means of Salvation and the privileges of the Church. On the contrary I will seek help and lend a hand for the slow and unwilling, according to the nature of the thing with the appropriate authorities or judges. When I in some way fail, and have been corrected and warned by those over me, I will with God's aid, make amends and put it to right.

All of this…I bind myself to as a true priest, and will creditably, according to my greatest ability, obey without neglect, without deception and angry strategems, as truly as God helps me, to life and soul.

Rudman then would have given his episcopal blessing:

God strengthen and comfort you always in this. Amen.

The Ordination was then announced by Rudman in these words:

And I, by the appointment which has been entrusted to me, by this commission of his Church on behalf of God, entrust to you the Order of Priest. In the Name of the Father, and of the Son, and of the Holy Spirit. Amen.

The other two Swedish priests who had been standing with Rudman before the altar, inside the Communion rail, then all together prayed the Lord's Prayer while all the priests laid their hands on the kneeling Falckner. The use of the Lord's Prayer as consecratory had a long tradition in Sweden and was a prominent feature also of the Baptismal Order. It had been a feature of the rite in the 1535 ordination proposal of Martin Luther.

Then followed a collect led by Rudman:

O eternal and merciful God, dear heavenly Father, who through the mouth of your beloved Son, our Lord Jesus Christ said, The harvest is plenteous but the laborers are few; pray therefore the Lord of the harvest that He send laborers to his harvest, and by whose words we understand that we cannot obtain right-minded and faithful Teachers, except by your merciful hand: we therefore pray with our whole heart, that you would deign to gracefully look upon this your servant, whom we have ordained to your service and Office of a Priest. Give him your Holy Spirit so that he may creditably and with power be able to do your holy work, teach and admonish with all humility and wisdom, so that your Holy Gospel may remain among us forever, pure and unadulterated, and bear for us the fruits of salvation and eternal life. Through your Son, Jesus Christ, our Lord. Amen.

Rudman then read the words of 1 Peter 5: 2-4 as a Benediction:

Tend the flock of God that is in your charge, not by constraint but willingly, nor for shameful gain but eagerly, not as domineering over those in your charge but being examples to the flock. And when the chief shepherd is manifested you will obtain the unfading crown of glory.[68]

The 1571 Order assumes that the Eucharist would normally follow. It seems reasonable to assume this since Svedberg mentions that it was a public service and since Swedish priests did not commune themselves when they celebrated the Eucharist. Thus Rudman would have worked for more than year without receiving Communion, and with thoughts about returning to Sweden, may not have known of another opportunity.[69]

The importance of the public celebration of the Eucharist in connection with the Ordination is well explained in the World Council of Churches 1982 statement, *Baptism, Eucharist and Ministry*:

A long and early Christian tradition places ordination in the context of worship and especially of the Eucharist. Such a place for the service of ordination preserves the understanding of ordination as an act of the whole , and not of a certain order within it or of the individual ordinand. The act of ordination by the laying-on of hands of those appointed to do so is at one and the same time invocation of the Holy Spirit (*epiclesis*), sacramental sign, acknowledgment of gifts and commitment.[70]

In this case the Luther hymn, "To God the Holy Spirit Let Us Pray," in the Olavus Petri translation, was sung as an Introit. Being so well known, the Germans could have sung it in their own language and the Swedes in theirs. Certain to be sung was the Hymn of Praise, "*Allenaste Gud*", "All Glory be to God on High," the versification of the Gloria from Luther's Deutsche Messe; Luther's versification of the Creed, "We all believe in one true God"; a Gradual hymn associated with the church year, and hymns during the distribution.

The lessons would have been chanted as would the collects and the Preface with the standard Easter Preface, and Words of Institution.[71] The Sanctus, Pax, and Agnus Dei would have been sung along with the Lord's Prayer. A variety of choices from the hymnals published by Rudman could have included Rudman's version of "Jesus Priceless Treasure" or any of the seven other hymns he had written or translated from German and published in Philadelphia three years earlier.

Sandel, as the host, was surely the celebrant of the Mass and Björk the preacher, with Rudman reading the Epistle. Bishop Svedberg tells us that Björk used as his text, Romans 10:15, "And how can men preach unless they are sent?"[72] Justus would have naturally received Communion as directed by the rubrics.

Unfortunately we have no eyewitness account of the Ordination. The episcopal residence of Bishop Jesper Svedberg in Skara burned down twice and with it went many valuable letters that are now beyond recovery. What we can do is imagine what may have happened on one of the most significant days in the history of Christianity in America.

ॐ 6 ॐ

The Ordination Certificate

As if by divine Providence, Justus Falckner's original ordination certificate turned up on the pastor's desk at St. James Lutheran Church, 73rd Street and Madison Avenue in Manhattan, one day in 1925. Actually it had been in the New York congregation's care since Falckner's death but had gone unnoticed. The original congregation was called Trinity but changed its name to St. Matthew's in 1826, by which time it had become a German-speaking congregation. In 1827, one of St. Matthew's pastors, Frederick Christian Schaeffer, withdrew from the congregation and founded St. James English Lutheran Church.

He took not only some of the more progressive members of St. Matthew's but apparently the ordination certificate too. In 1925, when the pastor of St. James, the Rev. Dr. William F. Sunday, recognized the certificate along with some other documents from colonial days, he had them placed in the vaults of the library of the Lutheran Theological Seminary at Gettysburg. St. James Church eventually merged into Holy Trinity Church at 65th Street and Central Park West, while St. Matthew's, after several moves, eventually merged with Messiah Church in Inwood at the northern end of Manhattan and ministers still on Sherman Avenue and 204th Street.

The discovery of this long-sought document was front-page news in New York. The *New York Times* ran a two column headline on May 5, 1925, announcing, "Long Lost Church Documents of Colonial Days found by Cleaning Women in Rubbish Heap." The article noted that "Possibly no document has been so diligently and persistently sought for by historians and investigators as this diploma…as its historical value to the Lutheran and Protestant Churches can hardly be overestimated."[73] Indeed it shows textually that the Ordination occurred, and seems to be the first such document in American history. It is written in Latin and signed by

Rudman and the other two Swedish priests, noting the date of the Ordination on the 24th and the signing in Philadelphia on November 25, 1703. Its existence shows that Superintendent Rudman was following Swedish Church regulations where it is recorded: "After the Ordination, the ordinand shall receive his ordination certificate (literally *priest letter*) from the Bishop in which his legal call and consecration shall be witnessed."[74]

There had been Roman Catholic ordinations in Spanish Florida as early as 1674, but the first in the thirteen colonies would be in Baltimore in 1793. The first Anglican ordinations were held in 1789 as the Protestant Episcopal Church was established. The first Dutch Reformed ordination was held as early as 1679, when four Dutch ministers ordained Petrus Tesschenmaacker for service in New Castle, Delaware. The first Presbyterian ordination was that of Jedediah Andrews in 1701 at Philadelphia. The Puritans of New England had ordained regularly since 1629 in a localized rite in which ordination and installation/induction/institution were combined in one service that was valid only in a particular local congregation.[75]

What made these latter Protestant ordinations different was the lack of one presiding official and a sense of Ordination into the Catholic Church. Falckner's Ordination was remarkable both because of its obvious catholic intent and its episcopal orientation in line with the historic western sacramental tradition. It was very carefully arranged with the canonical three priests who shared orthodox doctrine as participants. It was an act of the Catholic Church, as represented by a suffragan bishop and not an act of a single congregation to fill a vacancy. It was an affirmation of the apostolic faith. It was the first Lutheran Ordination outside of Europe and the first Ordination of a German in America. The Tranquebar Mission would ordain the first Protestant pastor in India, also the first non-European Lutheran, the catechist Aaron, in December, 1733 according to the rite of the Church of Denmark.[76]

The next Lutheran ordinations in America would be that of John Casper Stoever, Sr., and John Casper Stoever, Jr., performed by Pastor Johan Christian Schultz alone on April 8, 1733 in

Providence (Trappe) Pennsylvania. It was clearly seen as an emergency measure since only one pastor participated and no description of the service survives.[77] On August 14, 1748, just before the Ministerium of Pennsylvania was convened for the first time and as the new St. Michael's Church was dedicated in Philadelphia, John Nicholas Kurtz was ordained and called to the rural congregations in Tulpehocken, Pa. This was the first of many German Lutheran ordinations to be held under the auspices of this early synod. In addition to Henry Melchior Mühlenberg as the presider, three other German pastors took part as well as the Dean of the Swedish Ministerium, Johan Sandin of Swedesboro, N.J. and Pastor Gabriel Näsman, pastor of Gloria Dei Church, Philadelphia.[78] The next Ordination at which a number of Swedish priests took part was on June 10, 1860, when the constituting assembly of the Augustana Evangelical Lutheran Church, the church body that developed from the 19th century Swedish emigration, ordained three Norwegians and five Swedes.[79]

The parchment ordination document itself is in a remarkable state of preservation and measures 17" wide by 12" high. It is in the hand style of Andreas Rudman and it follows the standardized form used at Swedish Ordinations at the time.[80] Its rather ponderous retelling of the Old Testament story of salvation is a reminder that even though the Hebrew Bible was rarely read at Mass, it was often a sermon or study topic

A translation was first made by Dr. John G. Glenn of Gettysburg College in 1947. In the Falckner tercentenary year, Mary Margaret Ruth, a former Latin teacher and now (2003) a seminarian at the Lutheran Seminary in Gettysburg, working with Dr. Maria Erling of the faculty, and in consultation with Dr. Timothy Wengert of the Lutheran Seminary at Philadelphia, made a new translation, published here for the first time, that eliminated some of the inconsistencies in the earlier translation.

God Himself, the Establisher and Preserver of Holy Ministry, first discharged the office of preaching in Paradise and raised the first parents, deceived by the devil in disguise, for the hope of salvation by the promised Seed of the woman, that he would tread upon the head of the serpent. Nor is there any doubt that Adam had instructed his children as to how they ought to preserve their faith in the Promised Seed. Before and after the flood, there existed lamps of the restored Church and heralds of righteousness, Noah, Abraham and other ministers of the Divine Word. And after the promulgation of the law by Moses, already from then on, for a time of amendment, there were priests and Levites who enlightened the people of God by teaching and by exemplary life. However, since numbers of Levitical priests often executed this their duty rather negligently, it pleased God not only to censure their morals and degenerate life through the prophets, but also, when the time for the Church was nearer, for the Virgin Birth and the Nativity of the promised Seed, to put forth more clearly, by a succession of prophecies, the divine mystery for the restoring of the human race.

For in the New Covenant, by his own ordination, God distinguished between the teachers and those who heard, and guarded his order against the rank of the devil and the malice of the world. John the Baptist, by the order of God, assumed the office of preacher, whom Christ himself succeeded, who dipped in the water of Baptism, was publicly inaugurated into this office. Since it was necessary for Christ by his passion and death to redeem salvation and to ascend into the heavens, as soon as he had assumed the office of teaching on the earth, he called twelve apostles, taught them his sacred things, and commanded them that they should go forth to teach all nations. To these, as equal to them, he sent seventy disciples that they might proclaim the Word to the inhabitants of the Jewish cities.

The promised Paraclete, the Holy Spirit, has fulfilled the duties of the ascended Christ. Hence, Paul in his speech to the elders at Ephesus says that these inspectors of the Lord's flock have been placed there by the Holy Spirit. From this we are taught that no one of his own accord ought to assume the honor (of a priest) without a divine call. For the ministers of the Church are ambassadors of God. But no one assumes for himself the role of ambassador without the authority of the one sending him. They are stewards of the mysteries of God; thus they are as master of the household, managers of deploying the goods of the Lord. Accordingly, they are to be censured who, neither waiting for a mission nor the approval of the Church and of those to whom it matters, seize an ecclesiastical office by private decision, or take it over by force, or buy it for a price, or who by blood relation or by marriage alliance, either effected or about to be effected for a benefice, or by fraud or by buying votes or by other improper means whatsoever, force themselves into or allow themselves to be forced into office by others. What has regularly been made known in sermons concerning the success of such who by lawful or unlawful means force themselves into the sacred order has been noted: "As is the call, so is the success."

But those who truly and legitimately have been called to this sacred office are able to enjoy a tranquil conscience and to remember their call not without singular consolation. And by it as a shield they are able to protect themselves against all weapons of adversaries. In their number has been assessed the most esteemed and the most excellent JUSTUS FALCKNER, a German, who through prayers and the imposition of hands has been initiated by rite into holy orders[82]. He has been designated on the 24th day of November of this year for the ministry of the Church. We ask [You] the Most High God that he might add success to the office and each day to increase the gifts given by him to the new minister to the glory of his Name, the wellbeing of the Church, and not for his personal gain.

At Wicaco, on the 25th day of November in the year 1703.

Andreas Rudman
formerly Pastor of the Lutheran Church of New York in America
Ericus Biörk
Pastor of the Lutheran Church at Christiana in Pennsylvania
Andreas Sandel
Pastor of the Lutheran Church at Wicaco in Pennsylvania

7

Domine Justus Falckner
in New York and Albany

After a three-day journey, Justus arrived in New York City where he made the following entry in the Church Book that Rudman had begun in 1702:

> In the Name of Jesus. In the year 1703 on the second of December, I Justus Falckner, born in Saxony, Germany, at Langen-Reinsdorf, in the district of Zwickau, came to Philadelphia, thence to New York, after previous invitation. On the Third Sunday in Advent [December 12] I delivered two sermons in the Lutheran church here. I did the same on the Fourth Sunday in Advent.[December19] Thereupon I was received by the Consistory of the Christian Protestant Lutheran Congregation as their regular pastor and teacher.[83]

A Latin prayer follows in which Justus prays that God would be with "your lowly and feeble laborer with your special grace. In You, Lord I have hoped, let me never be confounded. Strengthen me in my vocation…"[84] It was a prayer that he would repeat in one form or another for the next twenty years as he journeyed up and down the Hudson and to the western hills of New Jersey. He is now the pastor or *Domine* as the Dutch called him.

At this time there were just three congregations: one in Manhattan, one in Hackensack, New Jersey and one in Albany county. Because of ice on the river he would not get to go to Albany until the spring. Right now there was plenty to keep him busy in Manhattan. The church building that dated from 1676 was located at the southwest corner of Broadway and Rector Street, the property stretching down to the Hudson River. It was just south of the newly erected Trinity Anglican Church at the end of Wall Street. A report to the Amsterdam Lutheran Consistory described it in this way:

The church we fear will be demolished by the first heavy storm; it is more like a cattle shed than a house of God, only two windows are in the building, one is back of the pulpit, and the other directly opposite. As the church is not paved, but merely floored with loose boards, some long, others short, one cannot pass through it without stumbling.[85]

A more detailed description of what it would have looked like is found in this footnote in the *Protocol of the Lutheran Church in New York City*:

The baptistery (Dutch: *doophuis*) in Dutch churches was that portion of the church building which we usually speak of as the chancel. It was separated from the congregation by a *doop-hek* or baptistery screen, of one to several feet high. The high pulpit was in the center, usually against or near the wall. At or near either side wall was a pew or two; the pew(s) on one side was for the elders; the pew(s) on the other side for the deacons. In front of the high pulpit and in the center of the baptistery was the Communion Table.[86]

While the membership had been somewhat reconstituted during Rudman's tenure, many had wandered away to the folds of the Dutch Reformed or the now official Anglican Church. Yet there were some distinguished leaders. Major Jan Hendrick deBruyn was one of the elders. In 1665, he, along with Jan Cloet and Jurrian Theunissen Tappan, invested in the purchase of a plot of land from the native Americans called Caniskeek. This land was later to become the town of Loonenburg/Athens, the center of Falckner's up-river ministry. deBruyn had also been an elder in the Albany congregation when Jacob Fabritius was pastor there. Another elder was Andreas van Buskirk whose large extended family was the backbone of the Hackensack congregation. His son Laurens van Buskirk was overseer and church master. Samuel Beekman was the *vooleser* and *koester*, or precentor/lay reader, who led the singing and read a sermon when the pastor was absent.

Justus was able to live with a man and his wife whose business was to carry freight up and down the river. The man's name was Pieter Pietersen van Woglom van Utrecht. He had owned land in what is now the center of Albany, knew people all over the valley, and gave Justus free transportation on his one-masted sloop "Unity" whenever duty called. The fact that Justus could live with him for several years proves the appropriateness of his nickname, *Soogemakekeyk*, or "So-Easy."[87] Another deacon was Hannes Lagrancie, a third-generation Huguenot whose father had served with de Bruyn on the Albany church council. Everyone spoke Dutch although the ethnic background of deBruyn was probably Norwegian, and van Buskirk, Danish. The work here was already different from that in Pennsylvania. It would be multicultural from the very beginning. In New York people of many sorts lived together rather than in segregated enclaves.

By February he could visit the congregation in Hackensack, New Jersey, about seventeen miles northwest of Manhattan. Here on the 27th he baptized three children, one of which was the son of Laurens van Buskirk. These were his first official "pastoral acts" and they begin the roll in the ledger that is still in the possession of St. Matthew's Lutheran Church in Manhattan.[88] This *Kerken Boeck* is a gold mine of information for genealogists and Falckner's entries show a profound personal concern for each person, often including a short prayer beside an entry. Thus after another Baptism in the Manhattan church on Easter Monday, 1704, he writes: "O Lord! Lord, let this child, together with the three above named Hackensack children, be and remain engrossed upon the book of life through Jesus Christ. Amen." [89]

Another typical prayer is: "O God, let this child be and remain a child of salvation through Christ. Amen." Or in 1705 for the daughter of Arie of Guinea and his wife Jora, both free African members of the Manhattan congregation, "Lord, merciful God, who look not upon the person, but from whom different people who fear you and do right find favor, let this child be clothed in the white robe of innocence and righteousness, and so remain through the grace of Christ, the Savior of all mankind. Amen"[90] While African persons were already members of the Danish Lutheran congregations in the Virgin Islands, this may be the first documented Baptism of a person of color in a Lutheran parish on the mainland.[91]

On Easter Sunday in 1708 a Carolina Native American slave was baptized and given the name Thomas Christian. The sacrament was administered in the presence of the congregation in Manhattan after the candidate had been publicly catechized by Justus. He was a slave in the household of Justus' host, Pieter Woglam. On January 27, 1712, an African slave of Jan van Loon's was baptized at Loonenburg and given the name Pieter Christian.[92] He was an adult since he was born in Madagascar about 1680.[93] He later was married twice to Palatine women (Anna Barbara Asner, 1714; Elizabeth Brandemoes, 1716). Seven children are recorded from the second marriage as baptized at Loonenburg. All of them would have been free.[94]

No doubt such baptisms were made easier by a provincial law that kept slaves with their masters even after their baptisms despite the Pauline injunction in Galatians 3:28.[95] Yet the fact that people of all backgrounds were members of the congregations is significant at this very early stage of colonial history.

The marriages and baptisms are available in an English translation published by the Holland Society in 1903. In addition to these registers, in the original there are lists of those who were admitted to Holy Communion, those who were dismissed, a burial register, a listing of church officers, and an inventory.[96] In the Church Book we can follow the missionary traveling up and down the Hudson to baptize, confirm, bury, marry and celebrate Holy Communion in central farmsteads. There is a certain irony in the strength that such house worship produced, since Governor Peter Stuyvesant in trying to eliminate the Lutherans from New Netherlands had forbidden them public worship but had allowed them the right "to practice their religion in their own homes."[97] Here Justus' piety was helpful with close personal relations and a worship style that was intimate and sustaining. Despite strenuous efforts, new church buildings were not built in Albany county and Manhattan during his lifetime. But the churches were so strengthened by his ministry that after his death buildings were dedicated in Manhattan and Loonenburg and fourteen congregations could claim him as their pastor.

The names in the Church Book are confusing. The patronymic usage was just being introduced and Falckner often adds a "sen" to names to indicate who was the father. Since the parishioners came from so many different countries, systems were fluid. Albert Bratt came from Norway bringing a surname with him but he was often called by his patronymic, Albert Andriessen. He is also called, "de Noorman," *i.e.*, The Northman. Some of his descendents are called Bratt and Braite while the descendents of his son, Jan Andriessen are called Jansen! One of his sons was nicknamed "van der Zee" because he was born during a storm at sea and thus his family are called Vanderzees. Sometimes Falckner calls them Hallenbeck, and sometimes uses only patronymics such as "Caspersen" (son of Casper).[98]

Justus wrote to August Francke back in Halle in May, 1704, and described his situation:

....after much persuasion, also prompting of heart and conscience, I am staying as regular pastor with a little Dutch Lutheran congregation, a state of affairs which I had so long avoided. I was publicly ordained in Pennsylvania by the Swedish Lutheran Ministerium and I received permission from my Lord Cornberry, the resident English Governor. It is evident that God, also here in the wilderness, wishes to plant the glorious cardinal doctrines of God's universal grace in Christ, of the universal restoration of the entire human race through and in Christ, of the blessed and unspeakable mystery that God is made manifest, of which the so-called Lutheran church above others is a custodian.

God gave me grace that I learned the Dutch language in a short time so that I now at times actually preach thrice a week. In Albany there also live some brethren of the Augsburg Confession; here they also have a small church, whither with God's help I shall travel this month, in which church, because those of the English church also go with them, I shall preach in Dutch and English. My auditors are mostly Dutch in speech, but in extraction are mostly High-Germans. Also Swedes, Danes, Norwegians, Poles, Lithuanians, Transylvanians, and other nationalities, although the entire country here is occupied by people of every sort. Verily our God is a mysterious God who can say to the wilderness, "Be cultivated!"[99]

It was the second week in May when the "Unity," captained by "So-Easy," left Manhattan for the dramatic four-day journey up to Loonenburg (Athens) and Albany. The town of Albany was dominated by the Dutch Reformed Church in the center and Fort Frederick on the hill. The Lutheran church building was thirty-five years old and was located on South Pearl Street. It had suffered from thirteen years of deferred maintenance and the members were so widely dispersed that while Justus could baptize, and celebrate Holy Communion he could not assemble officers for the congregation until the next June.

For the next four years he would live for the fall, winter, and spring in Manhattan, visiting Hackensack once a month and then by Pentecost visit the northern congregation, remaining during the summer. There he made his headquarters in the home of Jan van Loon, Jr. at Loonenburg.[100]

In October of 1704 the Church of England clergy of the middle colonies gathered for a convocation in Manhattan. The Rev. Evan Evans, the dynamic Welsh rector of Christ Church, Philadelphia, knew Justus and advised him to apply to the Society for the Propagation of the Gospel for support. Writing out the petition himself, Evans stated that he had known Falckner for four years and that his

> ...life & conversation is unexceptionable & suitable to the sacred Character he bears in the Church of God. He is a University Schollar & hath upon all occasions applied himself to his studys with care and diligence since his coming to America. He preaches to his Congregation twice every Sunday, & frequently visits the Lutherans in Albany, where he exercises the offices of his sacred function. He is in very good esteem (as I am credibly informed) amongst the people of his Congregation, but they being few in number, cannot allow him a suitable support for the comfortable discharge of his duty.[101]

It was signed by all of the nine other Anglican priests in attendance including Justus' neighbor at Trinity Church, William Vesey, the Bishop of London's representative (Commissary) in the province. It was indeed true that Justus was a scholar. Not only do we know of his studies at Halle and Leipzig and of his hymns and the Adult Catechism but we have in the Library of the Lutheran Theological Seminary at Philadelphia a copy of a Greek-Latin Dictionary to the New Testament that he owned with his name inscribed.[102]

Unfortunately the petition was not granted even though the Society gave support to Andreas Rudman as the rector of Trinity (Anglican) Church, Oxford, Pennsylvania and later to Joshua Kocherthal for his work with the Palatines. Perhaps it was not personal but tactical. The SPG was a new organization with limited resources and was succeeding in luring upper class French Huguenot parishes and Dutch Reformed churches into the new official Anglican fold. The Lutherans were mostly rural and less visible and did not rate the highest mission priority.[103] It is tempting to think how different church history in the Hudson valley would have been if Justus had become a regular SPG missionary.

Justus Falckner's first entry in the New York Church Book

∽ 8 ∾

Correspondence with the
Amsterdam Consistory

Since the language in all of the congregations was Dutch, it was
natural that Justus would carry on an extended correspondence
with the Lutheran Consistory of Amsterdam. However it was not a
propitious time for the Dutch. They were sitting in the middle of the
War of Spanish Succession that was raging between France and
Great Britain (1702-1713), sometimes with foreign troops on their
borders. Being a minority themselves and under suspicion for
catholic tendencies, the Consistory was not always in a position to
offer a great deal of assistance.

The letter that the congregation sent on November 10, 1705,
tells us a great deal about their situation.

We the Pastor, Elders, and Deacons of the Evangelical
Protestant Congregation adhering to the unaltered Augsburg
Confession at New York and surrounding places, wish grace
and blessing in and through Christ to...all worthy members
of the highly laudable Consistory of the Evangelical
protestant Church adhering to the unaltered Augsburg
Confession, at Amsterdam...our Congregation has become
dispersed, the young people and many of the older ones have
gone over to the Reformed Sect, until three years ago, at our
request, a Swedish minister, Mr. Andreas Rudman from
Pennsylvania came over and remained with us only over a
year...by his zeal he had persuaded another person who had
already been living for some years in this country, to have
himself at our formal request and call, appointed as our
present regular Pastor. He is by birth a German, from
Saxony, where he studied Theology, and was according to
Christian custom and the usage of our Evangelical Church
ordained to the holy Office by the Swedish Lutheran
Ministerium of Pennsylvania on the 24th of November, 1703.

He has therefore been with us now for nearly two years, and fills his office in such a manner that neither we nor anyone else has rightly anything to remark on his life and work…

Our congregation here is very small, because its members are dwelling far and near throughout the country; the majority of them are poor…it would be a great service here to have a booklet in which, by means of short questions and answers the differences between Lutherans and the so-called Reformed opinions were exposed, every point thus concluding, "Therefore the Lutheran opinion is the better one."…

Our church building is very dilapidated and will not long be suitable for the holy service, so that we intend to decide to build a small new church if God will move more such good hearts as our Lutheran fellow-believers at St. Thomas [Frederick Church in the Danish Virgin Islands] in the West Indies have proved to be who sent us, as a beginning, three hundred pieces of eight some months ago… There is hope that this our congregation, if supported only a little at first, will in this Country rejuvenate itself as an Eagle and be an asylum to many wandering and erring souls.[104]

They had also written to the Swedes on the Delaware and the Gloria Dei parish meeting of May 1, 1706, reports that the wardens were designated to go around to each home and seek contributions for the New York congregation.[105] It would not be enough, but the funds were put aside, and the old building repaired until a new structure was finally raised in 1729 with the assistance of Daniel Falckner, Jr. and his Raritan congregation in New Jersey.

No response came from Amsterdam, even though the letter was received. But when Justus wrote again on December 12, 1711, he received a favorable reply:

…Resolved to send to him and to donate to the aforesaid congregation, one large folio Bible, 50 Psalters[hymnals], 50 *Paradijshofjens* (*Paradise Gardens*), and 50 Haverman's prayer books.[106]

Trinity Lutheran Church, Manhattan, built in 1729 on the site of the earlier church building used by Justus Falckner, at the southwest corner of Broadway and Rector Street, just south of the present Trinity Episcopal Church. This drawing, reproduced from Sachse's *Justus Falckner,* is based on a sketch made in 1740.

They would not go far but when they arrived in June of 1713 they were greeted with great joy and Justus wrote back to the Consistory with his gratitude:

> ...let the sound of David's harp, with which the lovely voice of the singing throng to the number of fifty will go well, ring out freely, and our hearts being strengthened, let us rejoice in the Lord...For certainly, there has until now been a spiritual hunger among many of this small congregation here for this food of their soul which they, each in his measure, draw from such holy and spiritual books...[107]

In October of the same year Justus wrote again to request a missal book, which he described as

> ...a church agenda, containing all the formularies, not only of confession, the sacraments, marriage, burial, etc. but also those of ordination in octavo, with good large print...[108]

The Consistory wrote back on July 30, 1714, and promised to send two Agendas and included 12 bound octavo psalters[hymnals] and 12 duodecimo ones. Justus wrote back to them on October 3, 1715:

> The poor little Lutheran church in New York having received the splendid, generous present of 24 psalters [hymnals] and two church agendas sent to it as so many new tokens of your Reverences' favor and affection toward your said small and humble sister, hereby express its due gratitude, praying the Lord, our Savior as the sole general Head of His Church, that He may richly reward such love on your Reverences' part.[109]

Since the end of the war things were better in the Netherlands. Why Justus asks specifically for the Ordination rite is unclear. Perhaps there were possible candidates for ministry in his congregations. The Consistory sent an extra agenda for Falckner to take on his journeys.

Finally on June 12, 1717, the congregation could write to thank the Consistory for a gift of one hundred Holland guilders that had been given towards the building fund and received personally in Amsterdam by one of their own members, Johan Michael Schütz.[110] While the support from Holland was never extensive it was constant. There were probably many more letters exchanged than have been preserved. After Falckner's death these contacts would result in the ordination and call of his distinguished successor, Wilhelm Christoph Berkenmeyer.

GRONDLYCKE ONDERRICHT
VAN
Sekere Voorname Hoofd-stucken, der
Waren, Loutern, Saligmakenden,

Christelycken Leere,

Gegrondet op den Grondt van de Apo-
stelen en Propheten, daer

Jesus Christus

de HOECK-STEEN.

IS.

Angewesen in eenvoudige, dog stigtlycke

Vragen en *Antwoorden,*

Door

JUSTUS FALCKNER, Saxe-

Germanus, Minister der Christelycken
Protestantsen Genaemten Lutherschen
Gemeente te N. Tork en Alban.en,
&c.

Psal. 119. v. 104. (God) n Woort maeckt my
Kloeck; daerom hate ick alle valsche Wegen.

Gedruckt te Nieuw-York by W. Bradfordt,
1708

Title page of *Grondlycke Onderricht* (*Fundamental Instruction*), Justus
Falckner's catechism published in 1708, printed in New York by William
Bradfordt. The only remaining original copy is at the Historical Society of
Pennsylvania in Philadelphia.

❧ 9 ☙

"Fundamental Instruction" (1708)

Since there was no response to the congregation's request for a small book of questions and answers in 1705, Justus decided to publish one himself. His congregations were growing and there were so many questions that needed orthodox answers. During the winter of 1707-1708 he wrote an Adult Catechism with the exhaustive title page:

> FUNDAMENTAL INSTRUCTION in certain Principal Articles of the True, Pure and Salvific CHRISTIAN TEACHING, based on the Foundation of the Apostles and Prophets, of which JESUS CHRIST is the CORNER STONE, written in simple edifying QUESTIONS AND ANSWERS by JUSTUS FALCKNER, Saxon-German, Minister of the Christian Protestant Congregation called Lutheran in New York, Albany, etc.

It was printed at New York by the famed Church of England printer, William Bradford, and is the first educational volume to be published by Lutherans in the western hemisphere.

In the preface, written on Annunciation Day, March 25, 1708, Justus states why he is writing it:

> Since I have often been requested by different persons in our Christian congregation, to give them some direction from God's Word as proof and confirmation of certain Articles of Faith, which they have particularly been asked to explain and give reasons for, I took the occasion to undertake to write— in the peace of God, on account of the duty of the holy office in which God has placed me in my insignificance—in the Name of God.
>   ….I have concerned myself little or nothing with methods of worldly reason and wisdom, but have been

satisfied that it might be edifying for good and simple hearts.

....I have mostly printed the sayings word for word, as they stand in the holy pages, so that those who do not have a Bible, or cannot always get one for reading, or are unable to look up the verses, will be served...

....all that I have discussed in this little book should only be understood as conformable and agreeable to the said Christian Protestant Church, named Lutheran Church, teaching, confession and faith, which previously lived in my forefathers and parents, and also in my grandfathers, from my mother's and father's side, and my father, [all of them] honored by God to be useful *Pastors and Teachers* of his Church Militant; which confession of faith, by God's grace, convinced by his Word and Spirit, lives also in me, and will live to my final blessed end![111]

A listing of the twenty-one chapters in the Table of Contents gives a good idea of what is presented:

The Holy Scriptures, God, Creation, Angels, God's Providence, Man, The Image of God in Man, Free Will, Sin, God's General Grace, Election and Rejection, Christ, Repentance and Faith, Law and Gospel, Justification, Rebirth and Good Works, The Cross and Prayer, The Holy Sacraments: Holy Baptism and the Holy Supper, The Christian Church, The Three Principal States, The Last Things: Death, Resurrection, Last Judgment, Destruction of the World, Eternal Damnation, Eternal Salvation.[112]

The book was intended not only to defend the Church against the errors of the Reformed churches but to give a complete exposition of Christian doctrine suitable for an adult confirmand. First a question is asked, then a direct answer follows: yes or no. Then the Scriptural proof texts are cited. The book reads like a textbook in Lutheran orthodoxy. It shows how much Justus was at home in the theological debates of the previous century.

The rather extended condemnation of the fraction in the Eucharist is meant to defend the Lutheran insistence on wafers and the Real Presence of Christ in Holy Communion, against the use of "real bread" among the Reformed. The Minutes of the New York City Church Council tell us how the bread was prepared on October 1, 1725, and before:

> As to the consecrated bread, it was resolved that it should remain the same as in Pastor Falckner's time, namely, that the bread is to be pressed out with an iron.[113]

In other words only wafers would be acceptable at the liturgy of the Lord's Supper.

A direct attack on the Reformed belief that the Ascended Christ cannot be present in the Supper is found in Question 29 and its answer, in the chapter about the Holy Sacraments:

> Does the presence of Christ in the Holy Supper conflict with the truth of his human nature and with his Ascension into heaven, and his sitting at the right hand of God?
> Answer. No, for though the true Body and Blood of Christ is present in the Holy Supper, it is not there in a common natural manner, but in a supernatural, incomprehensible, though true nature and manner. And if one takes to heart what was said above about Christ's Ascension and sitting at the right hand of the Father Almighty, then one sees clearly that this makes the presence of Christ in the Holy Supper more certain than controversial.[114]

Such an answer was also intended to refute the famous "Black Rubric" in the 1662 edition of the Church of England's *Book of Common Prayer:*

> ...the natural Body and Blood of our Savior Christ are in heaven, and not here; it being against the truth of Christ's natural body to be at one time in more places than one.[115]

When Falckner answers the question about what constitutes the true Christian Church, his answer is essentially a quotation of the Augsburg Confession, Article VII:

> Answer. Where the Word of God is taught in its truth and purity and the Sacraments administered according to Christ's institution of them.[116]

His answer to what is the office of a regularly called pastor of the Church of God indicates his solid Lutheranism but also his definition for his own ministry:

> To teach the Word of God in its truth and purity, and to administer the Holy Sacraments as a true steward of the mysteries of God. To use the Keys of the Kingdom of Heaven according to Christ's institutions and will; and above all to set a good example himself, and to see to it that everything in the congregation may be conducted in an honorable and orderly manner.[117]

At the end of the book he appended three hymns. The first is a translation of Luther's Version of the Creed (*"Wir glauben all an einem Gott"*). The other two hymns are original compositions of Falckner and are meant to be sung before the Sermon.

There was no money to publish the adult catechism so Justus paid for it from his own meager salary and honoraria. We know this since the *Protocol* of the Church Council notes that on August 29, 1715, it was decided:

> …that the 24 books which the Consistory in Amsterdam presented to the Lutheran Church in New York are to be [sold] for the benefit of Pastor Justus Falckner…The receipts [from the sale] are to be used to pay for his expense and trouble in having a catechism printed at his own cost for the benefit of the congregation.[118]

The only extant copy of the *Fundamental Instruction* is owned by the Historical Society of Pennsylvania and kept in the adjacent Library Company of Philadelphia. A photocopy is in the Krauth Memorial Library of the Lutheran Theological Seminary in Philadelphia and in the New York Public Library. It is a small volume that was meant to be carried in a vest pocket. A portable theology was a new idea for the church's edification. It is one of the first books of adult Christian education to be printed in America.

In the Falckner Ordination Tercentenary year, an English translation of the *Fundamental Instruction* was published for the first time in cooperation with the American Lutheran Publicity Bureau. Pastor Martin Kessler of Danville, Pennsylvania, a native Dutch speaker and theologian, freshly translated the book and Prof. Johannes Boendermaker of Amsterdam provided a theological introduction to the text. Since so many of the issues of the past have been addressed in ecumenical dialogue, it is necessary to have some background before plunging into the work. Indeed, for many contemporary Lutherans, the issues Falckner identifies are not seen today as church dividing.

Yet for Justus it was vital to carve out an identity in a pluralistic culture. And for us it is instructive to see how seriously precise theological language is seen as fundamental to faith. It is not just a matter of doing good and loving one another that defines a Christian. It is also a strenuous intellectual pursuit grounded in the faith of the Scriptures and the faith of the community. In a society that wants to always answer, "Yes, but...." it is refreshing to hear Justus' clear "yes" or "no." The publication of such a work is a rebuke to the constant tendency towards pragmatism that runs like a red thread through Anglo culture.

In 1790 the state of New York counted 81 Dutch Reformed churches, 18 Episcopal churches and eight Lutheran churches.[119] While these numbers may be somewhat speculative, the percentages are right. The churches that Justus Falckner served were small and vastly outnumbered by larger and more affluent groups.

⧼ 10 ⧽

Kocherthal and the Palatines

The year 1708 saw several changes in Justus Falckner's life and ministry. Not only was his book published but his spiritual father, Andreas Rudman, died and was buried under the center aisle of Gloria Dei Church, not far from where Justus had been ordained.[120] At the time Rudman was serving as stated supply at both Christ (Anglican) Church in Philadelphia, and at Trinity (Anglican) Church, Oxford. Then his earlier mentor Johannes Kelpius died and the brotherhood dispersed. At the same time his brother Daniel, Jr. lost his position and land in Falckner's Swamp and finally made his way with his family to Somerset County, New Jersey, where he would be of some assistance to Justus in the New Jersey field. Finally Thomas Barclay came to Albany as chaplain for Fort Frederick and established an Anglican parish. Needing a place to meet he rented the Lutheran church since Falckner had been able to use it only a dozen times in the previous four years. Thus St. Peter's (Anglican) Church, Albany, was born in the old Lutheran church. Naturally this development reduced the possibilities for the growth of the Lutheran congregation whose center of gravity now moved south to the Loonenburg area.[121]

Justus already had responsibility for not only the major centers of Manhattan and Albany but groups in Loonenburg, Klinckenberg, Kinderhook, Coxsackie, Claverack and New Hamburg (Pieter Lassen's) along the Hudson River. In addition there was the New Jersey congregation in Hackensack.[122] Some idea of the size of the groups may be gained from the fact that one half of the salary was paid by the Manhattan congregation and one half was provided equally between Albany and Hackensack.[123]

In England the Bavarian Lutheran pastor, Joshua Kocherthal, had shepherded a group of refugees from the German area known as the Palatinate to London with the hope of settling in America. The King of France had ravaged the Palatine border area as a part of the War of Spanish Succession and the inhabitants were looking for a

64

...rch in Langenreinsdorf, Saxony, where
...us Falckner's father and grandfather were
...ors and where he was baptized Nov. 24,
...2. The lower part of the tower was built
...re 1467; the upper part in 1727. *Photos by
...tor Christian Freyer.*

Stained glass window by D'Ascensio Studios in Muhlenberg College Chapel shows Falckner as a student in Germany. *Photo courtesy of Muhlenberg College Public Relations.*

rtists' conceptions of alckner's ordination, based 1 Julius Sachse's book, *Justus Falckner*, include the cket illustration of Delber lark's *The World of Justus alckner* (above) and the ained glass window by ayne Studios in First utheran Church, Albany ght). Inaccuracies in these epictions are discussed in hapter 15 of this book.

REV. ANDREAS RUDMAN

JUSTUS FALKNER

ORDAINED IN 1703 TO BECOME THE MINISTER OF THE DUTCH LUTHERAN CHURCH IN NEW YORK

Sacri Ministerii Stator et conservator DEUS
parentes a personato deceptos diabolo, ad spem Sa...
esset. Nec dubium est, qvin Adamus Liberos ...
Ante et post diluvium, instaurata Ecclesia lamina
et post latam legem, jam inde a Mose, ad correct...
vitæ prælucerent. Qvoniam vero negligentius ho...
tantum illorum mores vitamq corruptam per prop...
nativitate promissi seminis abessent, eo clarius, ...
fœdere ordinatione in sua distinxit Deus Doctores
tus est. Johannes Baptista, jussu Dei, concionatoris munus au...
inauguratus est. Christum autem, cum oporteret passione et m...
suum in terris susceperat, 12 Apostolos vocavit, eosq su...
res 70 discipulos misit ut prædicarent Civitatibus
ptus. Hinc Paulus in oratione ad Presbyteros Ep...
neminem sibi ipsi, sine divina vocatione honorem (:
partes Legati absq Legantis Auctoritate; Sum...
norum Domini. Culpandi proinde sunt, qvi nec missio
et privato arbitrio, Ecclesiasticum munus capessunt,
sive conciliata, sive adhuc concilianda beneficiis, seu
ipsi, aut ingeni patiuntur per alios. De suiqn ta...
sermonibus celebratur: Qvalis vocatio, talis ...
conscientia et vocationis suæ, non sine singulari
tela, tueri possunt. In horum numero censendus
qvi per preces et manuum impositionem vitæ sacri...
um designatus est. Deum T. opt: Max: roga...
dies magis magisq augere, in nominis sui glor...

Vicario die 25 Novemb:
Año 1703.

Justus Falckner's ordination certificate, written in Latin, is dated November 25, 1703, the day after the ceremony, and signed by Andreas Rudman, Ericus Biörk and Andreas Sandel. The parchment document measures 17

primus in Paradiso concionandi munere fungebatur, primosq
promisso mulieris semine, erigebat, quod serpentis caput contriturum
statuerit, quomodo fiduciam in promisso semine reponere deberent.
eo praecones extitere, Noah, Abraham, alijq verbi Divini ministri
tempus, fuere Sacerdotes et Levitæ, qui populo Dei, doctrina et
officium sæpenumero executi sunt sacerdotes Levitici, placuit Deo, non
arcere, sed etiam, quo propius Ecclesiæ tempora a partu virginis et
rum Successu proponere reparandi generis humani mysterium. In novo
litoribus, insigniterq hunc ordinem adversus diaboli & mundi malitiam tuta-
est; qui Christus ipse successit, qui aqua baptismatis tinctus ad id munus publice
erij humani redimere salutem atq in cœlos ascendere, simul ac docendi munus
edocuit, quibus quoq mandavit, ut exirent docturi omnes gentes. His suppa
is: Christi in cœlum assumpti partes explevit promissus Paracletus Spus
ait eos gregis Dominici inspectores a Spu Stô positos. Ex quo docemur
:) sumere debere, nam ministri Ecclesiæ sunt legati: Ast nemo sibi sumit
omi mysteriorum Dei, ab hero itaq domus constituendi dispensatores Do-
Ecclesiæ et quorum interest, adprobationem expectantes ex proprio ausu
per vim occupant, aut pretio emunt, aut cogitationes vel affinitatij
, vel emendicatis suffragiis, vel quibuscunq aliis pravis artibus, sese ingerent
er fas et nefas, ordinis sacro se ingerentium, notum est, quod passim
Qui vero legitime ad sacrum hoc munus vocati sunt, tranquilla frui
tione, recordari, eaq tanq clypeo, se contra omnia adversitatum
eximius et Præstantissimus JUSTUS FALCKNER. Germanus
sacris initiatus die 24 Novemb: hujus Anni ad Ecclesiæ ministeri-
it Successum officii addere, et dona a se novo ministro data, in-
lesiæ salutem, nec non propinum emolumentum.

Andreas Rudman
antehac Past. Eccl. Luth. Neolboracensi in America

Ericus Biörck
Past. Eccl. Luth: ad Cranam in Pennsil.

Andreas Sandel
past. Eccl. Luth: ad Vicam in Pensylv.

inches wide by 12 inches high. See Chapter 6 and the Appendix of this book for a full discussion of the certificate and its history. *Original in the Archives of the Lutheran Theological Seminary at Gettysburg.*

Copia s.   New york October 27. 1704.

Reverend Brethren;

This is to certifie that I have known the Reverd.
Mr. Justus Falckner, the present Lutheran Minister at
New york, for four years last past, whose life & conver-
sation is unexceptionable & suitable to the sacred Character
he bears in the Church of God. He is an University Schollar
& hath upon all occasions applyed himself to his studys with
care & diligence since his coming to America. He
preaches to his Congregation twice every Sunday, & frequent
ly visits the Lutherans at Albany, where he exercises the
offices of his sacred function. He is in very good esteem
(as I was credibly informed) amongst the people of his
Congregation, but they being but few in Number, can
not allow him a suitable support for the comfortable
Discharge of his Duty. Therefore I humbly recommend him
to yor. pious consideration, not doubting of yor. care in re
presenting his case to my Lord of London & the Honble.
Society for the Propagation of the Gospel in these Parts.

We believe this Testimony to be true   Evan Evans

Hen: Nicols   Rōt Owen
Will: Vesey   John Barlow
John Sharpe   Thos: Moore
John Talbot   T. Prischard
                       Willm Uegnhart

The Reverend Clergy of the Church of Engeland
conven'd in the City of New york present.

The original I have sendd to Mr. Mecken Chaplain
to his Royal Highness Prince George of Danemark
in his Lutheran Chappel in St. James, the 18 octobr.
1704, by one student Mr. Thearson, together with
a letter to ye said Mr. Mecken.

Justus Falckner's personal copy of a letter from the Rev. Evan Evans and nine other Anglican clergy recommending him to the Society for the Propagation of the Gospel for financial assistance. *Original in the Archives of the Lutheran Theological Seminary at Gettysburg.*

on Church, Athens, N.Y., one of 14
ongregations served by Falckner, was
s place of residence in the final years
 his ministry. Present building was
onstructed in 1853. Plaque honors him
 its first pastor.

Top and bottom: Views across Hudson River from Athens (Loonenburg) toward presumed area where "Gospel Hoeck" was located. Center: Albertus Van Loon house, built 1724. He was one of the rivermen who transported Justus Falckner on his pastoral journeys. *Photos by Martin Kessler and Glenn C. Stone.*

peaceful refuge.[124] Queen Anne took pity on these "poor Protestant Palatines," providing free passage to New York with the idea that they would receive free land in turn for developing it.

Leaving England on the "Globe" in the fall of 1708, the first group of Palatines arrived in New York on New Year's Day, 1709. After a four-month delay in Manhattan they settled on the Quassaick Kill (Newburgh). They had been accompanied on their journey by the new Royal Governor, Lord Lovelace, who made sure that they were settled. Among other things Kocherthal was given a land grant and a site for a church building. However the Governor died a few months later and the financial subsidies were interrupted. The new settlers began to squabble among themselves and in the confusion Kocherthal was designated to return to London and present their dilemma to the Crown.[125]

Now Justus had a new group to give pastoral care to until Kocherthal returned. At the same time he had for the first time a colleague in the work on the Hudson. While Kocherthal was away, Justus baptized his newborn daughter, Louisa Abigail, on February 28, 1710, since his wife, Sibylla Charlotta, had not been able to make the journey back to England.[126]

Nine months later Kocherthal returned. So many Rhine-landers had left their homeland, both because of the severe winter and the war, that many had been stranded in Rotterdam. The British government chartered unused troop transports and brought 15, 000 to England in the summer of 1710. Some went to Ireland, others joined the British military, some Roman Catholics were deported, and some set off for North Carolina. About 1200 families were selected for settlement in New York, now that a new naturalization law made it easy to settle in the American colonies.

The "Wonder Fleet" composed of eleven ships[127] docked in Manhattan but the Palatines were soon moved to Governor's Island until a suitable location could be chosen for the proposed project of making tar and naval supplies for the British Navy. That location turned out to be a small tract in the village of Saugerties, and a large tract of land which belonged to Robert Livingston on the east side of the Hudson including the present Germantown, N.Y. It was about ninety miles north of Manhattan. By October of 1710 the Palatines were in their new locations, three hamlets on the east bank and two on the west. The agreement was that each family would get forty acres after they had earned enough to pay for their transportation and the costs of being fed.[128]

The spiritual care of these people was not left to chance. The Society for the Propagation of the Gospel re-ordained a German Reformed minister, Johan Frederick Haeger as a missionary to the Palatines. And of course Kocherthal ministered to everyone, including 140 converts from Roman Catholicism who found it desirable to become some sort of Protestant.[129] As Roman Catholics in a Protestant colony they would have had slim economic possibilities.

Already in July of 1710 when the "Wonder Fleet" was still on Governor's Island, Haeger wrote to the S.P.G. to complain about the competing effects of the combined efforts of the Lutheran pastors Falckner and Kocherthal:

> As I did sincerely intend, so had I hopes of transporting this people [the Palatines] into the Church of Christ as by law established in England and with all imaginable success; but after my landing I found that the Lutheran minister in this country had made already a separation and administered the Holy Sacrament to such of his confession as arrived in the ship before ours; persuading them that they ought to stick to that, in which they were bred and born; which Mr.Kocherthal after his arrival confirmed also, in so much that the separation between the Reformed and the Lutheran is fully made, which I did oppose with all my might and power.[130]

Justus had learned something from his experiences in Albany and from writing the adult catechism. It was important to make clear distinctions if a pastor wanted to retain his flock. Nowhere was the problem with the Reformed and some of the Anglicans clearer to the usual churchgoer than in Holy Communion. By communing not only were the communicants strengthened in faith but they were publicly renouncing Calvinism.

Haeger settled on the east bank on the Hudson, in the "capital" of the Palatine community, the village of "Queensbury" (East Camp/Germantown) in Livingston Manor. Kocherthal settled on the west side at Newtown, present West Camp. There was plenty of pastoral care and pastoral acts for both clergymen. Kocherthal was so preoccupied with his newest Palatines that Justus took over the work in the original settlement of Quassaick.[131]

With the Palatines came a change in the direction of the ministry. Both the congregation in the town of Albany and the congregation in Manhattan lost members while the outskirts to the south of Albany grew. Now Justus began to spend the entire winters in the northern area and the summers in Manhattan and New Jersey.

The first recorded pastoral act in Loonenburg is the Baptism of Maria, daughter of Jan van Loon, Jr. and Rebecca Hallenbeck, in 1711 in home of Jan van Loon, Sr. This was the official foundation of Zion Church in Loonenburg, now called Athens, although some gatherings seem to have been held there since 1706. In that same year of 1711, the estate of Jan van Hoesen who had died almost fifty years earlier was settled when his oldest son Jurgen van Hoesen died. The division of his land on the east side of the Hudson, directly across from Loonenburg led to the development of Claverack. One of the beneficiaries of this apportioning was Frank Hardik, Justus' future father-in-law.[132]

The tar-making project never really got off the ground. The provincial government was unwilling to support it and the Palatines were farmers who wanted to work the land. As Delber Clark described it:

> When the call came to go to the woods and peel bark from a strip one-fourth of the way around the base of a pine tree, and up as high as their chins, and the number of trees was endless, they rebelled.[133]

They claimed that the terms were different from what they had agreed upon in London. They asked to be resettled in the Schoharie Valley. The Governor disarmed them and quickly ended the "May Rebellion." It was not a good beginning for the summer of 1711.

What ended the project was what was happening across the Atlantic. In the summer of 1712 the anti-war Tories took over the English government and slashed all military spending. By the next spring, on April 11, 1713, the War of Spanish Succession, or as it was often called, "Queen Anne's War," had ended. Already by September 12, 1712, the provincial government had felt the cuts so drastically that they stopped all food rations for the Palatines. Some of the people began to disperse immediately. Others remained in the original settlements and still others wanted to move as group to a new location. After they had constructed a road from Schenectady to the Schoharie Valley, one hundred Palatine families left for the new area in March of 1713.[134]

Kocherthal had succeeded in building a small church in Newtown (West Camp) and made trips both to the Schoharie Valley and to the east side where he made use of the house that Haeger had built and used for worship. Haeger had organized a congregation related to the Church of England but had trouble getting a church erected at Queensbury because of the opposition of Robert Livingston. Livingston's father had been a Puritan clergyman in England who had lost his position with the restoration of the monarchy. Having married a Dutch woman and being a member of the Dutch Reformed Church in Albany, he had no interest in assisting the missions of the Church of England. He managed to delay the construction of the new Anglican church in Albany for two years. At last he even arrested the masons to halt construction.[135] When the Anglicans persisted, he encouraged the Dutch Reformed to build a larger church. They did this by digging a trench around the old building and building a larger structure over the old one. Then they took the old church apart and carried it out the doors. In the process they missed only three Sundays at their site.[136] They were thus able to open their new building before the Anglican church was ready for use.

Still Haeger managed some success. In 1710 he reported to the Society for the Propagation of the Gospel that he had 600 communicants and in 1714 he said there were 888 communicants in eight settlements in the counties of Albany, Dutchess and Ulster, and in the Schoharie Valley. At that time he said that 148 Palatine families had conformed to the Anglican Church and 73 families were Lutheran. Just a year later he counted 392 Palatine families of whom 54% were related to the Anglican ministry, showing an increase in both numbers and percentages.[137]

While Kocherthal had received the promise of a glebe in Newburgh and a stipend from Governor Hunter, these funds stopped when all of the financial support was terminated to the Palatine community in 1712. He wrote to the Society for the Propagation of the Gospel with a promise to try to induce his flock to conform to the Anglican Church. Already in 1710 he had expressed the same ecumenical willingness and had sounded out "…our Lutheran Palatines to know how they were disposed towards a Union with the Church of England, but find most of them averse to it; however I hope to bring them to it by degrees."[138]

By 1714 the SPG reported that since he was not an "official missionary" of theirs because of his Ordination as a Lutheran pastor, they could not accept him on a stipendiary basis. However they did grant him £ 20 "…in consideration of his great pains and poor circumstances--he having disposed many of his people to conform to the Church of England--and for his encouragement for the future, it not being consistent with the Society's rules to make him a Missionary."[139] In addition to his congregation in Newtown/West Camp, he visited Lutherans in Queensbury/Germantown across the river, settlers in the Schoharie Valley (1714) and in Rhinebeck (1715).[140]

Another direct result of the dispersion of the Palatines was the founding of a congregation in the mountains of western New Jersey above the Raritan River. Falckner was in the home of a freed slave, Arie van Guinea and his wife Nora, whose children he had baptized in Manhattan, to organize a congregation as early as August 1, 1714.[141] After the death of Justus, his brother, Daniel, Jr.

would serve these congregations until his retirement in 1734.[142] The four congregations that developed here in the New Germantown/ Raritan area, (Pluckemin, White House, Potterstown (Rockaway) and Fox Hill) were unified by Henry Melchior Muhlenberg as Zion Church in New Germantown. This congregation is today the oldest continuing Lutheran congregation in New Jersey. Since the First World War the community has been known as Oldwick.[143]

Another developing field was Remersbach/ Remmerspach /Ramapo in what is today called Mahwah, New Jersey, and Suffern, New York, straddling the border between the two. In 1715 Justus organized a congregation here which now made three parishes in the area for him to visit every summer. Sometime after the Revolution part of this congregation dissolved into the Dutch Reformed congregation in Mahwah, but Christ Lutheran Church in Suffern continues to serve today, as a legacy of Falckner's ministry in the area.[144]

❧ 11 ❧

Marriage to Gerritje Hardick

It was not until May 26, 1717, that Justus was married. In his own Church Book he recorded:

> On Rogate [Fifth Sunday after Easter] Sunday, did the Reverend William Vesey, Commissary and Preacher of the English Church in New York, on license from His Excellency Robert Hunter, at that time Governor of the Province, marry and solemnize in the bonds of matrimony, me, Justus Falckner, Pastor of the Protestant Lutheran Congregation, and the honorable virgin, Gerritje Hardick, born in the Province of New York, Albany County; at my house in Little Queen Street. I leave you not, Lord Jesus, bless me then.[145]

The groom was forty-four years old and the bride twenty-five. Justus had confirmed her just five years earlier. She had been baptized at the Dutch Reformed Church in Albany. It seems unusual that the marriage was not held at her parents' home in Claverack and that Kocherthal was not the officiant. But in that case Justus would have had to read his own banns and he had no home there, whereas there was a parsonage that he could move into in Manhattan.

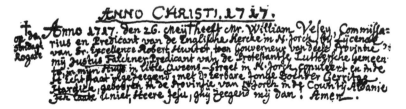

Falckner's entry of his own marriage in the Church Book

Other difficulties also seem to have surfaced with Kocherthal. We know that he was more inclined to work with the Anglican Church and Haeger than was Justus. Kocherthal had also married Haeger to Anna Catharina Rohrbach just the year before.[146] Kocherthal was also involved in trying to secure his glebe in Newburgh although the parishioners there were more ready to give the land to Justus since he had been providing them with regular pastoral care. Actually the land in Newburgh would have been well centered for Justus' ministry if he had received it and his wedding made the possibility of a permanent home more attractive. The discussion about the 250 acres of land here probably muddied the waters between them.[147]

It was natural for Justus to ask William Vesey to officiate since their church buildings faced each other and they had been friends for a long time. It also did not hurt that Vesey was the leading clergyman in the province and the representative for the bishop of London.

After a summer in Manhattan, and a winter up the river at the home of Jan van Loon, Jr., in Loonenburg, Justus and Gerritje returned to Manhattan in the summer of 1718. Here their first child, Anna Catharina was born. His record in the Church Book notes the simple facts: "Born, July 17, Tuesday night at half past ten, at New York in Little Queen Street." She was baptized the following Friday. The godfather was Pieter, son of Pieter Pietersen van Woglom and the godmother was a cousin of Gerritje's, Katharina van Hoesen.[148] Anna Catharina would marry Hendryk Van Hoesen on October 22, 1740, and have six children: Jan H., Gerritje, Tanneke, Justus H., Hendricus, and Maria. All of their names appear on the baptismal roll of Zion Church in Loonenburg.[149]

Justus and Gerritje's family would add another daughter on May 5, 1720, while they were still in Loonenburg. She was baptized as Sara Justa on May 8 in Loonenburg. The witnesses were Jan Casperse, his son Casper Hallenbek and Rachel Casperse. Sara married Nicholas Van Hoesen on December 22, 1738, and the couple had seven children: Jan, Justus, Cornelis, Gerritje, William,

Nicholas, and Jannetke. Again all of them are listed on the baptismal roll of Zion Church.

In the very year that Justus died, 1723, his son Benedictus was born and baptized at the homestead that Justus had received from his father-in-law, "Preuwen Hoeck." The Baptism took place on April 11, 1723, with godparents Jan Hardick and Anna Catharina (daughter of Daniel Falckner, Jr.) Hardick. The choice of the name is fascinating. According to local tradition he should have been named Frank after his maternal grandfather. Perhaps Justus was so happy to have a son late in life that he recalled the aged Zechariah's canticle at the circumcision of John the Baptist, "Blessed be the Lord God of Israel…"(Luke 1:68). Benedictus married Jannetje [Falkner?] and had at least two children: Justus and Marya.[150] Again the records are at Zion Church in what is called today, Athens, N.Y. With this many descendants from three children it is easy to see how Falckner relations have always been members of Zion Church even into the 21st century.

The homestead of "five and twenty mogens of woodland" was about fifty acres of land that had not yet been cultivated in Claverack, on the east side of the Hudson, across from Loonenburg. Since the original name of the estate was "Preuwen Hoeck" it seems as if there was a prune orchard there.[151] Since Justus was not a farmer the woodland was especially valuable for the family. Justus, Gerritje, Anna Catharina, and Sara Justa moved into the house there in the fall of 1721. It must have been especially welcome for Gerritje who was now close to family and friends instead of being isolated from them in Manhattan. It was at about the center of the upriver Dutch population and in fact the strongest concentration lived in Claverack. Some seventy families lived within a radius of eighteen miles. Justus refers to it as "Gospel Hoeck" or "Gospel Corner" and his records often mention, "the church in my house."[152]

That same fall saw the arrival of Daniel, Jr.'s daughter, Anna Catharina. She may have been fleeing the isolated conditions of the Raritan hills or more probably her home situation. In any case she was confirmed by Justus on January 4, 1722, and married Gerritje's brother, William Hardik on April 22, 1722.[153]

The constant travel that preoccupied Justus must have been difficult for his family. He was never ahead of the needs and there was always much more to do than one person could do. His salary was so meager that the honoraria and in-kind gifts he received from pastoral acts were a necessity for survival. In the very year that he was taking his own money to pay for the printing of the adult catechism, his salary was in arrears as the Protocol reports.[154] After his death the letter that the congregation in Manhattan wrote to the Amsterdam Consistory reports that the financial situation is still bleak:

> ...The churches and congregations of the Lutheran and Unaltered Augsburg Confession in the province of New York and thereabouts...are not in a position to pay a proper yearly salary to such a pastor, not to speak of the expenses of maintaining our churches...[155]

Before his marriage Justus was fortunate to be able to board with parishioners, who to a certain extent took care of him as a member of the family. After his marriage he was on his own to provide for his own family. His work and his income suffered if he did not travel, yet when he did, he had to leave his wife and young children.

The household was enlivened by the use of a multiplicity of languages. The local Hudson River Dutch was tinged with Frisian and Danish and so not quite what was spoken in the Netherlands.[156] When Palatine visitors came to Gospel Hoeck, the language changed to German and when English speakers arrived, the official language of the colony was used.

❧ 12 ❧

The van Dieren Controversy

In 1716 Johan Bernhard van Dieren arrived in Manhattan. He was a tailor from East Prussia without much formal education. He was a master of the theological cliché and with his emotional piety he soon made friends in the congregation and in the city and at Hackensack. He had arrived by way of London where he met one of the German court preachers at the Savoy Chapel, Anton Wilhelm Boehm (1673-1722), who lent him books and encouraged him. Now he was convinced that God had called him to minister with the Gospel to the dispersed Germans in America. Neither Justus nor Kocherthal were impressed, and neither offered to ordain him. Finally he went to Philadelphia and tried talking to the pastor of Gloria Dei, Jonas Lidman, but got no encouragement. Yet since Justus was away from Manhattan for three-quarters of the year, van Dieren's supporters increased.[157]

With what turned out to be a fatal illness, Kocherthal was not traveling as much now as earlier and the burdens for Justus increased. Finally, the almost abandoned inhabitants of the Schoharie Valley heard about van Dieren and wrote two letters in May, 1721, to Justus requesting that he be ordained for them. Justus suggested that van Dieren visit the Swedish churches on the Delaware for counsel. The written answer from the Dean of the Swedish congregations, Andreas Hesselius, also pastor at Holy Trinity, Christina (Wilmington) was not encouraging:

> As to Bernhard van Dieren I have been able to discover nothing from him except his singular zeal (would that it had been more wisely directed)…I only dread that much injury may result…Only he is worthy of the ministry who is ordained unwillingly.[158]

He was not only ignorant, and unsure of his doctrinal bearings, but impolite and forward as well. Van Dieren got no further with

Hesselius than he had with Lidman.

All of this did not seem to lessen his fanaticism. On August 19, 1721, Justus married him to Maria, the daughter of one of the more uncooperative Manhattan church officials, the tailor Johan Schuetz. It was Schuetz who had been in Amsterdam and had received one hundred Dutch guilders for the Manhattan Church's building fund but who delayed turning the money over to the Church Council for a year after his return. The newly married couple then set off on their "mission" to the Schoharie.[159] The injury that Hesselius had predicted was not long in coming.

While he told the people at Schoharie that he had been ordained, he kept asking Justus to ordain him. These two stories eventually caught up with each other. In addition his method of celebrating Holy Communion was an odd mix of Lutheran and Reformed usages, with his own ideas enriched by some Eastern orthodox customs. Forgetting the opposition which Lutherans maintained to breaking the bread, when he came to the Institutional words, *broke it,* he "...laid aside the book, and broke the long loaves or the round cakes into four parts, Then he cut them into disks with the knife and broke the disks into smaller pieces."[160] The result of this was that everyone was offended, the orthodox Lutherans and those who had Reformed backgrounds.

Fifty-two members of the Schoharie congregation wrote a protest letter to Justus. Van Dieren had exposed himself as an unscrupulous fraud. The congregation dispersed but then looked to a Dutch Reformed minister for pastoral assistance. Van Dieren fled back to Manhattan and resumed his tailoring but did not give up his clerical ambitions.[161]

On September 6, 1723, Justus writes to the congregation in Kamp (East Camp/Germantown) advising them not to call van Dieren as their pastor.[162] He was obviously a constant irritant for Justus, fueled both by the chronic lack of clergy and van Dieren's unsuitability. By 1730 the same congregation together with the Palatines from Rhinebeck would request a missionary from the SPG, promising a forty-acre glebe, a salary and a willingness to use the

Book of Common Prayer in German. They were sent books but no pastor.[163]

As late as 1727 van Dieren was still trying to function as a clergyman. First he made trouble in Albany as William Christoph Berkenmeyer, Justus' successor, explains in a letter of June 6, written to the Church Council in New York City:

> Thank God the commotion which was made by a vagabond preacher among the brethren in Albany turned out to be of little importance. Most of the people have renewed their friendship [for the Church], and every one has subscribed to the [new] building. Those who framed that shameful call still wander about in order to get subscriptions for a salary of 5 pounds. But they are laughed at...[164]

Later in the same year he convinced his van Buskirk friends in Hackensack that they should call him as their pastor. This called forth a formal protest from Berkenmeyer who was, by now, well aware of van Dieren. He again called on the Swedish pastors on the Delaware for an opinion. A lengthy letter was signed by the same Jonas Lidman who had met him before and who was now Dean, as well as pastor at Gloria Dei, Philadelphia, together with three other Swedish priests: Samuel Hesselius, (Christina/Wilmington), Petrus Tranberg (Racoon/Swedesboro, N.J.), and Andreas Vindrufva (Pennsneck/Pennsville, N.J.). The letter reported on October 31, 1727:

> You did do very ill, dearly beloved Friends, in taking up with such a pretended priest; because if ordained, it was not done lawfully. He was with us about his Ordination, but we denied it him for two reasons. First, that we had not such Authority, that we could ordain priests. Mr. Rudman indeed did ordain Mr. Falckner, the late priest of the Lutheran Congregation at New York; but he was made a Suffragan, or a Vice-Bishop by the Archbishop of Sweedland. For the second, That we thought him not Qualified for that Sacred Function.[165]

The comments by the Swedish priests only reinforce the special role that Rudman played in the Ordination of Justus. The van Dieren affair is interesting because it shows the mirror opposite of Justus' ordination. The matter of the proper authority to ordain and the qualifications of the candidate were to be constant subjects of debate until the organization of the first synods.[166]. Many a schoolmaster saw the possibility of earning a few shillings by preaching on Sundays and enlarged his resume to make it sound legitimate. Some became licensed lay preachers but others were simply con artists.

The Swedish priests then report that van Dieren subsequently went to see Anthony Jacob Henkel at Falckner's Swamp but that Henkel had also refused.[167] They conclude by saying:

> …You have done very well, dearly beloved Friends, in excluding him from the Service of your Church, and better you will do, if you hear him no more, since he is like to destroy your Congregation. Neither take up with such men, till they can show necessary Testimonies from some Consistory in Europe, of their lawful Ordination and likewise a good Conversation.[168]

By 1730, van Dieren is in Pennsylvania with a group of Dutch settlers at Neshaminy, in Bucks County. He is also known to have preached and administered the sacraments in Tulpehocken to the Palatines who had moved there from the Schoharie Valley in 1723.[169]

On November 5, 1734, Michael Christian Knoll who had come in response to Berkenmeyer's plea and had taken over the Manhattan and Hackensack congregations, wrote a letter to the Swedish pastors on the Delaware to warn them about van Dieren. He shows in even more detail the problems that Justus faced with this parishioner:

> …the man is so ignorant and stupid that he cannot even write a syllable of the native language without all kinds of mistakes. Actually, we have three letters of his in which are

78

1200 mistakes…He is an evil man, who by his lies ventured to nullify the appeal [to Amsterdam] made by Berkenmeyer and myself. He is an unscrupulous man, who wanted for his own possession the land given as a glebe to the Church in Hackensack. He is a hypocrite, for he would be at the same time head of our Church and the Calvinists, as though he were a pastor. He is a cruel man, permitting his Negro female slave to be tormented by hunger and tortured by labor day and night…[170]

Henry Melchior Muhlenberg reports that van Dieren wanted to join the Ministerium of Pennsylvania and be the pastor of the congregation at Upper Milford, Saucon, Pa. Putting it very charitably, Muhlenberg says: "The providence of God, whose footsteps we try to follow, did not ordain that this should be."[171] Van Dieren's will of November 12, 1750, identifies him as the pastor of the local Neshaminy Lutheran congregation.[172] It seems more likely that he was in fact still earning his daily bread with a needle and thread.

❧ 13 ❧

The Final Journey

The rigors and privations of pioneer life aged all of the clergy prematurely. Constant travel over non-existent roads on horseback in poor weather, lack of proper housing and insufficient salary, too little encouragement from abroad, and dealing with impoverished and uneducated parishioners, who were not always either generous or co-operative, made their life a constant challenge. For Justus, the last four years of his life meant that his workload was more than doubled, when first Kocherthal and then Haeger died.

Kocherthal had not been able to visit Schoharie in the summer of 1718 because of failing health. Through the winter of 1718-1719 he continued to grow weaker even though his responsibilities grew heavier because of the continued movements of the Palatine community. In the spring of 1719 he decided to return to England and seek help. But after officiating at a Baptism on May 14, he grew weaker and by June 24, 1719, he was dead. He had been born in Landau, Bavaria in 1669 and was thus three years older than Justus. He was buried at St. Paul's Church in West Camp (three miles north of Saugerties) where thirty-three years later his daughters raised a stone in his memory which calls him:

> …a true sojourner of the High-Germans in America, their Joshua, And a true Lutheran preacher unto them on the East and West side of the Hudson River…[173]

At about the same time Haeger was cut from further support by the SPG. With limited resources, he died in 1721.[174] He was younger than Justus, having been born in 1684. In his last days he warned his congregations about the dangers posed by van Dieren and advised them to seek new pastoral help from the Amsterdam Consistory.[175] In 1724, his successor in Schoharie, John Jacob Ehlig,

80

who used the Anglican rite in German, was also denied the salary of an SPG missionary.[176]

In 1722 Falckner indicates in the Church Book visiting the following places for pastoral acts:

January: Gospel Hoeck, Newtown (West Camp), Gospel Hoeck;

March: Klinckenberg (Loonenburg);

April: Queensbury (Germantown), Rhinebeck, New Town, Gospel Hoeck;

June: Raritan, N.J.;

August: Hackensack, N.J.;

September: Manhattan;

November: Albany, Tar Bush (Manorton), Queensbury, Rhinebeck, Queensbury;

December: Gospel Hoeck.[177]

This listing does not indicate how many services he conducted or how many sermons he may have preached at these or other places along the way. From the Raritan hills of New Jersey to Schoharie it was more than 150 miles and the indirect roads made the journeys even longer.

There are only a few entries in the Church Book for the summer of 1723 and Justus did not go to the Raritan parish that summer. He officiated at a marriage in Elizabeth Town [Elizabeth], N.J., on August 27 (Julian calendar) or September 7 and the last entry is dated September 4 (15 by our present calendar):

> ...baptized at Philipsburg [Yonkers] at the upper mill, in the house of David Sturm, Johan Peter, born in the middle of June, at the same place. Father, Peter Hentz; Mother, Maria. Witness: Johan Berger.

Justus is not feeling well on September 20 when he writes his will in Manhattan. The names of the witnesses suggest that he is in New York City.

In the Name of the Holy, Blessed and Glorious Trinity, Amen. The 9th (20th) of September 1723, I, Justus Falckner, Minister of the Protestant Lutheran Congregation in New York and Albany, being in indifferent health of body but of sound memory, considering the uncertainty of Life and the certainty of death...[178]

In a letter written by Johannes Sybrandt to the Amsterdam Consistory in 1726, he says:

> ...It so happened in the year 1723, on September 11/22, when I came to New York from the Bermudas, after a half-lost voyage, that there came to me Johans LaGrangsie and Carel Beekman, deacons of the above-mentioned congregation, who lamented that they were very uneasy and sad about the decease of their pastor Dom. Justus Valkenaar, Not knowing where they could get another.[179]

Thus since he wrote his will on September 20 and was reported to have just died by the 22nd it is probable that he died on September 21, 1723, the date of the commemoration of St. Matthew, the name by which his surviving congregation in Manhattan is known. He was surely buried in the graveyard of his Manhattan church, where his tomb undoubtedly lies under the skyscrapers of Rector Street.

From Langenreinsdorf to Germantown, from Philadelphia to New York and Albany, from the Raritan hills to Long Island, and up to the Schoharie Valley, his journeys make him one of the foremost missionaries in the history of the Church in America.

In 1703 there were three congregations: Manhattan and Albany, N.Y., and Hackensack, N.J. Twenty years later he was serving fourteen: Manhattan, Albany, Loonenburg (merged with Klinckenberg about 1719), New Hamburg (Pieter Lassen's), Quassaik (Newburgh), Queensbury (East Camp/Germantown), New Town (West Camp), Rhinebeck, Schoharie, Gospelhoeck (Claverack/Churchtown), Tar Bush (Manorton), Hackensack, N.J., Raritan, the mountain congregation, later Zion, Oldwick, N.J. and

Remmerspach/Ramapo on the border between New Jersey and New York at present day Mahwah/Suffern.

His journeys were apostolic, traveling from home to home with the Word and Sacraments. He lived in apostolic poverty, yet his fidelity to the Gospel allowed many to join him in the great throng of pilgrims who journey to that land where all nations and peoples are united in the realm of God.

Justus Falckner's official signature identifies him as a Saxon-German and "pastor of the Dutch Lutheran Orthodox Church at New York in America."

❧ 14 ❧

Falckner Hymns

The essential catholicity of Lutheranism is nowhere as evident as in its hymns. At the time of the 16th century Reformation a great many German poets and musicians contributed to a growing chorale repertoire for German congregations. These hymns were translated into the Nordic languages and other poets and musicians developed their own contributions to the participation of the congregation in Sunday worship. At the same time some of the Latin hymns were translated into the vernacular or continued in their medieval forms, especially the traditional sequences. Many pastors and poets contributed to the increasing number of evangelical hymns in northern Europe. Music was very much a part of the Mass and in fact a spoken liturgy was a rarity allowable only on the grounds of the poverty of the congregation. The simplest devotion would include the singing of a hymn. Hymns were regularly memorized as a part of the school curricula.

The Pietistic movement gave a new impulse to hymn-writers. The personal relationship of the believer to Christ could now also be explored in hymnody. The hymn-writers of Pietism sounded a call to repentance and new life for the Church. They emphasized sanctification and a sense of mission. August Francke himself was a hymn-writer. Both Kelpius and Rudman, Justus' spiritual mentors in America, were published hymn-writers.[180] Thus when Justus writes hymns during his student days in Germany, it was a usual rather than an unusual thing to do, although he seems to have had more ability than many others, and eventually was able to write in two languages.

His most famous hymn, *Auf! ihr Christen, Christi glieder*, in its original version had eleven stanzas. It was published in Francke's collection for the use of the orphanage at Halle, the *Geistreiches Gesang Buch* (1697). It may have been written in 1692-1693 during his year of study at Halle. It was originally sung to the chorale tune,

Auf, ihr Christen, Christi
Glieder! die ihr noch
hangt an dem Haupt; auf!
wacht auf! ermannt euch wie-
der, eh ihr werdet hingeraubt.
Satan beut an den Streit
Christo und der Christenheit.

2. Auf! folgt Christo, eurem
Helde, trauet seinem starcken
Arm, liegt der Satan gleich zu
Felde mit dem gantzen Höllen-
Schwarm: sind doch der noch
vielmehr, die da stets sind um
uns her.

3. Nur auf Christi Blut gewa-
get mit Gebet und Wachsam-
keit, dieses machet unverzaget,
und recht tapfre Krieges-Leut;
Christi Blut gibt uns Muth
wieder alle Teufels-Brut.

4. Christi HeeresCreutzes-Fah-
ne, so da weiß und roth ge-
sprengt, ist schon auf dem Sieges
Plane uns zum Troste ausge-
hängt; wer hier kriegt, nie er-
liegt, sondern unterm Creutze
siegt.

5. Diesen Sieg hat auch em-
pfunden vieler Heilgen starcker
Muth, da sie haben überwundē
frölich durch des Lames Blut.
Solten wir dann allhier auch
nicht streiten mit Begier.

6. Wer die Sclaverey nur lie-
bet, Fleisches Ruh und Sicher-
heit, und den Sünden sich ergie-
bet, der hat wenig Lust zum
Streit; den die Nacht, Satans
Macht, hat ihn in den Schlaf
gebracht.

7. Aber wen die Weisheit leh-
ret, was die Freyheit sur ein
Theil, dessen Hertz zu GOtt sich
kehret, seinem allerhöchste Heil,
sucht allein ohne Schein Christi
freyer Knecht zu seyn.

8. Denn vergnüg! auch wohl
das Leben, so der Freyheit man-
geln muß? Wer sich GOtt nicht
gantz ergeben, hat nur Müh,
Angst und Verdruß; der, der
kriegt recht vergnügt, wer sein
Leben selbst besiegt.

9. Drum auf! laßt uns über-
winden in dem Blute JEsu
Christ, und an unsre Stirne
binden sein Wort, so ein Zeugniß
ist, das uns deckt und erweckt,
und nach Gottes Liebe schmeckt.

10. Unser Leben sey verborgen
mit Christo in GOtt allein, auf
daß wir an jenem Morgen mit
ihm offenbar auch seyn, da das
Leid dieser Zeit werden wird zu
lauter Freud.

11. Da GOtt seinen treuen
Knechten geben wird den Gna-
den-Lohn, und die Hütten der
Gerechten stimmen an den Sie-
ges-Thon; da fürwahr Got-
tes Schaar ihn wird loben
immerdar.

The original version of *"Rise, O Children of Salvation"* as reproduced in Sachse's *Justus Falckner* from the *Zionitischer Weyrauch's Hügel,* the hymnal of the Ephrata community in Pennsylvania.

Meine Hoffung stehet feste. Julius Sachse says that in the manuscript copy there are two Scriptural references for the hymn's inspiration.[181] The first is Ephesians 6:10, "Finally, be strong in the Lord and in the strength of his might." And the second is 1 John 5:4,: "For whatever is born of God overcomes the world; and this is the victory that overcomes the world, our faith."[182] It bore the designation, "An encouragement to conflict in the Christian warfare."

The hymn became quite popular especially with those who dissented from the established churches because of its militant language. This emphasis is even stronger in the original than in the translation. Thus it appeared in the first book printed in German script in America, the hymnal of the Ephrata community, *Zionitischer Weyrauchs Hügel*, printed by Christopher Sauer in Germantown in 1738.[183] Among Lutherans in this country it was printed in the Lutheran *Kirchenbuch* (1877) and in English in the *Common Service Book* (1917) and the *Service Book and Hymnal* (1958).

It was first translated into English and reduced to four stanzas in the 19th century by Emma Frances Bevan (1827-1909). She published it in her 1858 *Songs of Eternal Life*.[184] It survives in slightly altered form as *Rise, O Children of Salvation* in the *Lutheran Book of Worship* (1978) as number 182. The tune to which it has been sung in America, "Unser Herrscher," fits well its martial spirit even though its composer is ironically enough one of the best-known composers of the German Reformed tradition.

Two other hymns are known from Justus' student days in Germany. *O Herr der Herrlichkeit* likewise appeared in the hymnal of the Ephrata brotherhood. Also, in the supplement to the Moravian Hymn Book of 1801, which appeared in 1808, No.1064 is an English language hymn whose second stanza is called, "If our lives for Him we Venture" which was originally written by Justus, according to Sachse.[185] The hymn's first line is: "In that glorious vest arrayed.". Since each stanza has four lines and the metre is 8888 it is not a translation of *Auf ihr Christen, Christi glieder.* The Moravian hymnal does not list authors but only indicates an original

86

German hymn with an asterisk. No hymns by Falckner appear in the contemporary Moravian hymnals.

Three other hymns by Falckner are known from his *Fundamental Instruction* of 1708 where they are appended to his catechetical text. The first of these is a Dutch version of Martin Luther's versification of the Nicene Creed, *Wir glauben all an einen Gott*. It is found in the *Lutheran Book of Worship* (LBW) (1978) as number 374, set to a traditional medieval plainchant from the 14th century. Justus would have known this hymn from both the German and Swedish liturgies where it was regularly used in place of a spoken confession of faith.

The other two hymns seem to be original compositions. It is indicated that either of these hymns is to be sung before the Sermon. The first one was translated by Martin Kessler and paraphrased by Kim-Eric Williams for the Falckner Ordination Tercentenary in 2003. The hymn has four stanzas that address the Holy Trinity:

> O God, eternal Lord of all,
> Come bless us as we humbly call,
> That by your Word and Sacrament
> We now may own your love's intent.
>
> O Lamb of God, Christ Jesus, Lord,
> Help us to heed your wond'rous Word.
> For we have gathered in your Name
> Our hope and heritage to claim.
>
> O Holy Spirit, Truth Divine,
> Come now to ev'ry heart and mind.
> May ev'ry act and ev'ry deed
> Unite our faith in word and creed.
>
> O hear us, Holy Trinity,
> O Father, Son, and Spirit, three,
> We pray together from the heart
> That we from you may ne'er depart.

It could be sung to any Long Meter tune, such as LBW No. 230, No.253, or No. 284.

The third hymn was almost indecipherable in the sole surviving copy of "Fundamental Instruction…", because it is the last page of the book and the ink has run together to blot out the letters. It has two unusually long stanzas, each with twelve lines. The 887 meter is difficult and it may be that that a standard chorale like LBW No.196 was repeated to fit in all the words.

Lord God, with grace your Spirit send
And in our hearts your truth now lend
   In this new world you give us.
Let not our lives conceal your power
But let our love express the hour
   Your Cross was raised to save us.
Turn us from sin and change our ways
That we may walk in all our days
   As bearers of your kingdom.
Then let us praise your mighty Word,
Give it success, let it be heard
   In every land and family.

How soon our days on earth are past,
Like clouds they flee, they do not last
   But your Word lasts forever.
O Spirit, send your gifts to us
Of peace, love, order, faithfulness,
   Renew us with your presence.
Build up our faith, open our eyes
To see the greed and printed lies
   That seek to overpower us.
O Holy Spirit, truest light,
Increase our vision, day and night,
   Until we reach your banquet.

The paraphrase was created by Kim-Eric Williams on the basis of a literal translation made by Martin Kessler in 2003.

ᔷ 15 ᔶ

Falckner Echoes
in the Following Centuries

In the year 1734, Justus Falckner's successor in Manhattan and Hackensack, Michael Christian Knoll, is already referring to him as "the sainted Justus Falckner."[186] Yet no notice seems to have been taken of him in 1803 at the centennial of his Ordination.

The next notice of him is from Jehu Curtis Clay, who was the first Episcopal priest to serve as rector of Gloria Dei Church in Philadelphia. In his *Annals of the Swedes on the Delaware* (1835) he has this amusing comment on Justus' ordination at Old Swedes church:

> This ordination by presbyters, instead of by a bishop, was the best their situation, or the circumstances in which they were placed, enabled them to obtain. A sister church wanted a pastor, and they had to decide between letting them go unsupplied, or giving them one with defective orders; or perhaps, they thought such orders would do for the Dutch.[187]

Clay's definition of apostolicity was not that of modern ecumenists Neither did he have access to the sources appointing Rudman to ordain or his later career as a stipendiary SPG missionary serving two Anglican parishes in Philadelphia . He would have been surprised to discover that Superintendent Rudman consecrated and named the Anglican parish in New Castle, Delaware, as Immanuel Church in 1706.[188] Actually Clay's opinion was not all that different from that of the Augustana Lutheran theologian Conrad J .I. Bergendoff, who doubted that Rudman had such authority and who in 1956 proposed that Justus had been ordained according to the non-episcopal structures of the Lutheran Church in the Netherlands.[189]

Beale Melancthon Schmucker, the famous Lutheran liturgical scholar and pastor of the 19th century, felt that the nationality of the ordinand made the situation questionable: ..."The Swedish Ministers and Provost[Dean] had received special authority to ordain a man named pastor to the Swedish churches. Since Falckner was not a Swedish pastor, they made bold to do so in Falckner's case."[190]

Yet Justus Falckner was not well known among 19th century church historians who emphasized the work of Henry Melchior Muhlenberg and events in Pennsylvania. Even in Athens, New York, where all of Justus' descendants had remained, there was uncertainty about just who he was. One of his descendants, U. Grant Van Hoesen in writing a history of Zion Church declared that both Daniel, Jr. and Justus were "...sons of a Lutheran minister in Holland."[191]

By the end of the 19th century, the Lutheran systematician and historian from Philadelphia, Henry Eyster Jacobs, was hoping that the *Fundamental Instruction* of 1708 could be translated into English and published in time for the Ordination Bicentennial in 1903. This would not happen for another hundred years but Julius Friedrich Sachse (1842-1919) did write the first biography of Justus Falckner in commemoration of the Bicentennial.

Sachse was the librarian and curator for the Grand Lodge of Pennsylvania Freemasons in Philadelphia. He was active in the Historical Society of Pennsylvania and one of the originators of the Pennsylvania German Society. He wrote a good number of works about historic figures in Masonry and was especially interested in the German immigration to Pennsylvania. He wrote a large book entitled, *German Pietists of Provincial Pennsylvania* in 1895.[192] .In this work published in Philadelphia he imagined the Ordination service for Justus Falckner and his 1903 biography was an enlargement of a chapter in this earlier book. He gave his new book the extended title: *Justus Falckner, Devout Pietist in Germany, Hermit on the Wissahickon, Missionary on the Hudson.* This title appeared in gold on the cover. On the inside title page, the book was further defined as: "A Bi-Centennial Memorial of the first Regular

Ordination of an orthodox pastor in America, done November 24, 1703 at Gloria Dei, The Swedish Lutheran Church at Wicaco, Philadelphia." It was published for the author and he explains on the same page that it was "Compiled from Original Documents, Letters, and Records at Home and Abroad." The book is richly illustrated.

This book put Justus on the theological and historical map. Theodore Schmauk published a long history of Lutheranism in Pennsylvania in the same year and incorporated the Sachse description of the Ordination verbatim.[193]

The good thing about this biography was that it made the name of Justus Falckner known and no church historian could then eliminate him. The unfortunate part was that Sachse included very few footnotes and was not above "creatively imagining" details when something seemed to need a fuller description. When he could not locate the original Ordination certificate he found the beginning words in an original letter that Justus had sent to Amsterdam and wrote in the rest according to what was usual in the Church of Sweden. With the use of trick photography he provided a "facsimile" that was impressive.

While this was in fact rather close to the original, which was not discovered until 1925, Sachse took credit for discovering the original and unwisely used the same Falckner wax seal beside each of the three signatures at the bottom of the certificate, giving the wrong date and the wrong titles to the participants.

He did the same with the Ordination service. Since there was no eyewitness account, he took a sample Swedish Ordination service of the 19th century, added some musical renditions by the Wissahickon hermits and told what psalms were sung, not realizing that the Swedish word for hymn is *psalm,* it being quite certain that no psalms from the Hebrew Bible were used. And of course the rite in the early 18th century was not the same as in the 1890's. Since he was hoping that the Lutheran Church of his time would recover more of its catholicity, he vested Rudman in chasuble and stole, and had Justus invested in a chasuble and stole. It was a charming and romantic description but it had no basis in fact. Sachse's lack of theological study made him strain for effect. At his funeral the newspaper announcement said that the rites were conducted by both a Lutheran and an Episcopal minister, as if to make sure that the Lutherans would finally get it right.[194]

By 1929 Luther D. Reed, professor at the Lutheran Seminary in Philadelphia, in designing the stained glass symbolism for Muhlenberg College Chapel in Allentown, Pa., selected Justus Falckner for one of the bays. It was an appropriate choice since Muhlenberg was at the time a Lutheran men's college that prepared quite a few of its graduates for seminary. The D'Ascensio glass studios imagined a young 18th century student for Falckner since no portrait of him exists. In the clerestory above appears an image of Gloria Dei Church in Philadelphia.

In 1937 the Board of American Missions of the United Lutheran Church in America produced a film about domestic missions and honored Falckner with the title, "Like the Thunder of the Sea"--taken from the last line of the last verse of his hymn, *Rise, O children of salvation.*[195]

In 1939 Paul Zeller Strodach, a literary editor for the United Lutheran Publication House, found it amazing that Falckner had worn an alb since he was in the process of trying to convince Lutheran pastors to wear cassocks, surplices and stoles.[196]

Just after the Second World War, a clergyman of the Episcopal Church, Delber Wallace Clark, wrote a new biography of Falckner. It was titled, *The World of Justus Falckner* and was published by Muhlenberg Press in Philadelphia (1946). Clark knew that there was something wrong with the description of the Ordination but was defeated by the thought of trying to locate and translate the Swedish records. One suspects that he may have also been charmed by the story since his footnote says: "This chapter is based entirely on Sachse's account in his book, *Justus Falckner.* While it may not be accurate as to facts, it represents as nearly as can be reconstructed the general picture of the ordination; and since it has become traditional it is reproduced to complete the picture of Falckner's life."[197]

92

Clark did a much better job of describing the Hudson River ministry than had Sachse. However he unwisely tried to reconstruct from the Church Book the trips that Justus took up and down the Hudson. This leads to a splitting up of themes and an overabundance of genealogical references that have limited value to those whose families are not mentioned. He shows his pastoral skills by occasionally taking a flight of homiletical fancy, as when he describes the arrival of Justus in Manhattan:

> No one but a saint or a fool would have tried to save the New York Lutheran church in the winter of 1703-04. History has demonstrated that if Justus Falckner was a fool, he was a fool for Christ, which is another way of saying he was a saint. [198]

By the time of the 250th anniversary of Justus' Ordination there was even more interest in the Ordination itself and his subsequent ministry. The original certificate had already been translated and published in 1947. The *1953 Yearbook: The United Lutheran Church in America* included an article by William H. Baar, "Justus Falckner Anniversary". The author embellished the Sachse account even more declaring that "… the drama of the occasion was heightened by the presence of Indians who had been attracted by the solemn procession into old Gloria Dei church…Last came Rudman in alb with crossed stoles and a resplendent cope."[199] Baar was pastor of Emanuel Church in New Haven, Conn., one of the more liturgically advanced churches in the denomination, and transposed the current usage of the Church of Sweden into the past as a lesson for the less observant brethren.

At its annual convention, the United Lutheran Synod of New York and New England held a "Service of Thanksgiving and Praise in Commemoration of the 250th Anniversary" at Battell Chapel at Yale University, New Haven,. on June 2, 1953. The service was loosely based on the Amsterdam Church Order and featured Abdel Ross Wentz, professor of church history at the Lutheran Seminary in Gettysburg, Pa., as the preacher. The surviving Falckner churches in the Synod were listed as: First, Albany; Zion, Athens; Christ, Germantown; St. Paul's, West Camp; St. Peter's, Rhinebeck; St.

John's, Manorton, and St. Thomas, Churchtown. St. Matthew's, New York City, was not listed since it had affiliated with the Missouri Synod in the 19th century, and the English language daughter of old Trinity, St. James, had merged into Holy Trinity at 65th St. and Central Park West.

For this occasion, Harry J. Kreider, Chairman of the Committee on Documentary History of the Synod and pastor of St. James' Church, Ozone Park, N.Y., wrote a new description of the ordination in a three-page addendum to the service. It was the first description that did not depend on Sachse. Kreider had obtained a copy of the Swedish 1571 Order and had it translated. This was a much more accurate description although he was not able to reconstruct the "solemn vow." He did correctly place the Ordination in the context of a Eucharist. The cover of the service pamphlet showed the imagined ordination, with the participants in wigs and stoles, a somewhat less liturgical scene than what Sachse had described. Kreider officially disclaimed this line drawing but that was not enough to prevent it from being used as the cover of the *1978 Yearbook of the Lutheran Church in America,* marking the 225th anniversary of the Ordination.

If delegates to the 1953 convention were confused it was understandable. Baar, as chairman of the event looked to an even fuller liturgical event than Sachse had imagined. Kreider, as the Synod historian provided the first realistic description, and the artist for the cover of the commemoration liturgy invented a scene that pleased no one.

Kreider's short pamphlet had a small circulation, being limited to the pastors, delegates and visitors to the convention of the Synod. The limited distribution was unfortunate since it really prepared the way for the present biography and unmasked many of the flaws in Sachse that had infected Falckner research since 1895. Thus when Mark Oldenburg wrote his dissertation in 1992 on "The Evolution of Ordination Rituals in East Coast Lutheranism, 1703-1918" he unwittingly remarked about Sachse's portrayal of Justus' Ordination, "His description has never been criticized."[200]

94

When First Lutheran Church in Albany finally dedicated its new building in 1954 it included a vivid stained glass portrayal of Justus' ordination. The church is a copy of the Chapel of the Abiding Presence at the Lutheran Seminary at Gettysburg and has a similar type of neo-Georgian windows. Unfortunately, the artist from Payne Studios in Paterson, N.J., used the Sachse description, misspelling Falckner's name as "Falkner." Rudman is shown wearing a stole and a chasuble is shown folded on the altar rail for Justus. Luckily the window does include a drawing of a Hudson River sloop of the type that Justus used to move up and down the river. The representation is placed in the lower portion of a window portraying the Resurrection. This was a masterful choice since the power of the resurrection is what motivates the mission and the missionaries of the Church.

In 1972 the 300th anniversary of Justus' birth was marked by a Eucharist at Gloria Dei, Old Swedes Church in Philadelphia. It was held exactly on his birthday, Wednesday, November 22 at 11:00 a.m. The committee that planned the Eucharist included Alan C. Freed, pastor of Good Shepherd Church, Dundalk, Md., Richard E. Bloomdall, pastor of the Lutheran Parish of West New York, N.J., and Glenn C. Stone, editor of *Lutheran Forum* of the American Lutheran Publicity Bureau. The preacher was the retired editor of *The Lutheran Companion* and distinguished hymn writer, E. E. Ryden. What is interesting in this celebration is how the latter three pastors all had a common background in the former Augustana Evangelical Lutheran Church, the church of the 19th century Swedish immigrants. The Church of Sweden connection was among the factors that drew them to Falckner.

The 275th anniversary of Justus' ordination was observed on April 22, 1978, at Gloria Dei Church in Philadelphia when the Lutheran Historical Society of Eastern Pennsylvania heard a lecture by Dr. Helmut T. Lehmann, professor of church history at the Lutheran Seminary. Dr. Lehman told the details of Justus' life and the story of the forged ordination certificate but wisely avoided any comment on the Ordination itself.[201]

The year 2003 has proved to be the most significant in the series of Falckner celebrations. Besides the publication of this critical biography and the long-awaited *Fundamental Instruction,* the Easter edition of the *Archives Advocate*, published by the Lutheran Archives Center at Philadelphia was entirely devoted to Justus Falckner. A celebration was held with the Bishop of the Upstate New York Synod, Marie C. Jerge, on October 26 at Zion, Athens, with the participation of George E. Handley, President of the Lutheran Archives Board of Directors in Philadelphia. As we go to press, another commemoration with the participation of the author of this book, Kim-Eric Williams is planned for Holy Trinity Lutheran Church, Manhattan, on November 22 in connection with a gathering of the Lutheran Historical Society of Greater New York.

On Sunday, November 23, clergy and members of the Southeastern Pennsylvania Synod of the Evangelical Lutheran Church in America and the Diocese of Pennsylvania of the Episcopal Church will come together at the Philadelphia Cathedral of the Episcopal Church. Both Lutheran Bishop Roy G. Almquist and Episcopal Bishop Charles E. Bennison will participate. The preacher is to be the Rt. Rev. Frederick Borsch, first holder of the Anglican Chair of Theology at the Lutheran Seminary at Philadelphia. A one-act chancel drama, "At the Door," written by the author of this book, is to precede the liturgy and set the historical stage for the Eucharist. Members of the Swedish Colonial Society will be present as well as representatives from all of the eight original Old Swedes churches. This will be the first gathering of the "Swedish Ministerium" since 1784.

In addition, a movement was begun in the Metropolitan New York Synod to memorialize the Evangelical Lutheran Church in America to add Justus Falckner to the list of commemorations in future liturgical publications, on the day after St. Matthew's Day, *i.e.,* September 22. Written by Pastor Glenn C. Stone and passed with variations by a number of synods, the resolution reads in part:

Whereas, the year 2003 marks the 300th anniversary of the ordination to the Holy Ministry of Justus Falckner, the first

Lutheran ordained in North America (November 24, 1703), and

Whereas both the ordination itself and Falckner's subsequent ministry hold great historical and contemporary significance for the Church...

Therefore, be it resolved (1) that the...Synod voice its gratitude to God for the life and ministry of this early leader of our Church in the Northeast, and urge its members to take the opportunity of this 300th anniversary to participate in commemorative events, especially in the month of November, 2003; and (2) that the...Synod memorialize the Evangelical Lutheran Church in America to direct that in any future revision of the Calendar of Commemorations published in its books of worship and otherwise commended to its members' observance, the name of Justus Falckner, Missionary, be included, for commemoration on September 22nd.

Following 20th century precedent the *2003 Yearbook* of the Evangelical Lutheran Church in America, has on its front cover a full color reproduction of the Justus Falckner window in the chapel of Muhlenberg College.

Afterword

This book probably began when I was a student at Muhlenberg College and looked up at the stained glass figure of Justus Falckner in the chapel, realizing that I knew very little about him. My interest was piqued when I began work as the translator for the Swedish Colonial Society's long term "Gloria Dei Records Project" in 1997. Among the bound manuscripts there I found not a full description of the Ordination but only a short note by Andreas Sandel that it had taken place. I was also fascinated to translate the appointment letter of King Carl XII for Andreas Rudman to be a Superintendent of the Church of Sweden in America. When I read Sachse it seemed intriguing but also esoteric. As the chaplain of the Swedish Colonial Society, I realized that this event should be celebrated in some way in the Delaware Valley during the Tercentenary year.

It was in the spring of 2002 that Glenn C. Stone contacted me and the President of the Lutheran Archives Center at Philadelphia, George E. Handley, to ask who was going to write the new biography of Falckner. An alternate proposal would be to republish the Clark volume. When I read Delber Clark's biography I realized that its organization and lack of use of subsequently published research made this an unwise choice. Since I was planning to spend the coming summer studying in Sweden and could use the resources at Uppsala and Skara, it began to seem as if I was volunteering to be the author of the new volume. When I considered my background as a descendent of the colonial Swedes in Pennsylvania, a former member of an Augustana Church in Massachusetts, and a priest of the Church of Sweden, it all seemed to make sense.

Especially helpful was Hans Ling of the Swedish National Board of Antiquities who personally did a great deal of research, and Uppsala professors Stellan Dahlgren and Hans Norman who read and commented on the manuscript. Peter S. Craig, the Historian of the Swedish Colonial Society and the Editor of the "Gloria Dei Records Project" commented helpfully on the text. He has kindly allowed us to use materials from that forthcoming multi-volume publication that will be copyrighted by Gloria Dei Church.

Especially valuable were the publications of the Documentary History Committee of the United Lutheran Synod of New York and New England and its distinguished historian, the late Harry J. Kreider. He was the sort of careful researcher that every diocese or synod needs to have as an official historian. In addition to his fine PhD. Thesis from Columbia, *Lutheranism in Colonial New York* (1942) he authored a *History of the Synod* (1953), and with Simon Hart issued *Protocol of the Lutheran Church in New York City, 1702-1750"* (1958). He saw to it that in 1948 Arnold J. F. van Laer's *The Lutheran Church in New York (1649-1772)* was published and cooperated again with Simon Hart in issuing *Lutheran Church in New York and New Jersey, 1722-1760* (1962).

Through my work with the Lutheran regional archives centers at the Krauth Memorial Library of the Lutheran Theological Seminary in Philadelphia and at Wagner College in Staten Island, New York, I was able to get copies of both the 1571 and 1686 *Church Ordinances* of the Church of Sweden and translate them from the original script. Thanks to archivists John F. Peterson at Philadelphia and John Daggan in Staten Island.

My good friend, Pastor Frederick S. Weiser, one of the leading scholars on Pennsylvania German culture and religion, made numerous helpful comments and personally wrote to Langenreinsdorf to obtain material about the Falckner family, and the National Library in Berlin to get matriculation information about the Falckner brothers and secure the right to duplicate a letter written by Justus. He has done the translations for all of the entries in the church books from Langenreinsdorf. Peter Christoph, the archivist of the Upstate New York Synod and a well-known researcher on Dutch colonial history discovered the details about Justus' death place and date. Glenn C. Stone was constantly supportive, a careful editor and advisor and secured the funding for and support from the American Lutheran Publicity Bureau for the publication.

Many thanks go to George E. Handley, who as President of the Archives Board, has managed a mass of small details and seen to it that 2003 will be remembered for a long time as the "Falckner Year." As a native of Quassaick (Newburgh), N.Y., he has both a personal and a professional interest in the project. His many comments on the manuscript have improved the final result. Martin Kessler's response made possible a new paragraph in the chapter on the *Fundamental Instruction*, and his translations of the second and third hymns from that work made possible my eventual paraphrases. Robert Nabom, professor of Dutch at the University of Pennsylvania translated the note from the Dutch Lutheran Church in Manhattan to Rudman. The travel grant from the Germanic Languages Department of the University of Pennsylvania to go to Sweden last summer made my first-hand research possible there.

I am grateful to H. George Anderson, Presiding Bishop emeritus of the Evangelical Lutheran Church in America, for writing the Foreword. Not every church body has been lucky enough to have had a distinguished church historian as its spiritual leader at a time when historic directions and ecumenical decisions were in flux.

At the beginning of the 21st Century all major churches in the United States are facing a chronic lack of vocations for parish ministry. May the journey of Justus Falckner inspire many to answer the call of the Spirit and the Church. None will have to travel over 1500 miles on horseback and river sloop in just one year as Justus reported doing in 1715, and while in the early 18th century there were no canons, constitutions or committees, yet the task was the same then as today

> … to build up the body of Christ by proclaiming
> and teaching the Word of God, by celebrating the
> sacraments, and by guiding the life of the community,
> in it worship, its mission and its caring ministry.
> *Baptism, Eucharist and Ministry* (1982)[202]

Kim-Eric Williams
Midsommar, 2003
Nativity of St. John the Baptizer

Appendix

Latin Text of Ordination Certificate

In view of the historic importance of Justus Falckner's ordination and the scholarly value of the document which attests to it, we offer here Dr. Timothy Wengert's transcription of the Latin text. The English translation in which Prof. Wengert, Dr. Maria Erling and Seminarian Mary Margaret Ruth cooperated, is published in Chapter 6 of this book, and a photo reproduction of the original appears at the centerfold of the book.

Sacri Ministerii stator et conservator DEUS IPSE, primus in Paradiso concionandi munere fungebatur, primosque parentes a personato deceptos diabolo, ad spem salutis promisso mulieris semine, erigebat, quod serpentis caput contritarum esset. Nec dubium est, quin Adamus Liberos suos instituerit, quomodo fiduciam in promisso semine reponere deberent. Ante et post diluvium, instauratae Ecclesiae lumina justitiaeque praecones extitere. Noah, Abraham, aliique verbi Divini ministri et post latam legem, jam inde a Mose, ad correctionis tempus, fuere Sacerdotes et Levitae, qui populo Dei, doctrina et vita praelucerent, Quoniam vero negligentius hoc suum officium saepe numero executi sunt sacerdotes Levitici, placuit Deo, non tantum Morum mores vitamque corruptam per prophetas arguere, sed etiam, quo propius Ecclesiae tempora a partu virginis et nativitate promissi seminis abessent eo clarius, vaticiniorum successu proponere reparandi generis humani mysterium. In novo foedere ordinatione enim sua distinxit Deus doctores ab Auditoribus, insigniterque hunc ordinem adversus diaboli et mundi malitiam tatatus [=tutus?] est. Johannes Baptista, iussu Dei, concionatoris munus auspicatus est; cui Christus ipse successit, qui aqua baptismatis tinctus ad id munus publice inauguratus est. Christum autem, cum oporteret passione et morte generis humani redimere salutem atque in coelos ascendere, simul ac docendi munus suum in terris susceperat 12 Apostolos vocavit, eosque sua sacra edocuit, quibus quoque mandavit, ut exirent docturi omnes gentes. His suppares 70 discipulos misit ut praedicarent Civitatibus Judaicis. Christi in coelum assumti partes explevit promissus Paracletus Spiritus Sanctus; Hinc Paulus in oratione ad Praesbyteros Ephesinos ait eos gregis Dominici inspectores a Spiritu Sancto positos. Exquo docemur neminem sibi ipse. Sine divina vocatione honorem (:sacerdoti:) sumere debere, nam ministrii Ecclesiae sunt Dei legati: Ast nemo sibi sumit partes [Ecclesiae *crossed out*] Legati absque Legantis Auctoritate; sunt Oeconomi mysteriorum Dei, ab hero itaque domus constituendi dispensatores bonorum Domine. Culpandi proinde sunt, qui nec missionem, nec Ecclesiae et quorum interest, adprobationem expectantes ex propria ansa et privato arbitrio, Ecclesiasticum munus capessunt, aut id, per vim occupant, aut pretio emunt, aut cogatationis vel affinitatis sive conciliatae, sive adhuc conciliandae beneficis, seu fraudibus, vel emendicatis suffragiis, vel quibuscunique aliis pravis artibus sese ingerunt ipsi, aut ingeri patiuntur per alios. De successu talium per fas et refas, ordinis sacro se ingerentium, notum est, quod passim sermonibus celebratur: Qualis vocatio, talis successus. Qui vero legitime ad sacrum hoc munus vocati sunt tranquilla frui conscientia et vocationis suae, non sine singulari consolatione, recordari, eaque tanquam types, se contra omnia adversitatum tela, tueri possunt. In horum numero censendus est Severimius et Preaestantissimus JUSTUS FALCKNER germanus qui per preces et manuum impositionem rite sacris ordinibus initiatus die 24 Novemb[ris] huius Anni ad Ecclesiae ministerium designatus est. Deum T[uum] Opt[imum] Max[imum] rogamus velit successum officio addere, et dona a se novo ministro data, indies magis magisque augere, in nominis sui gloriam ecclesiae salutem, necnon proprium emolumeniam.

Wicaco die 25 Novemb[ris]
Anno 1703

Andreas Rudman
ante hac Past.Eccl.Luth.
NeoEboracensis in America

Ericus Biörck
Past.Eccl.Luth: ad Christiam in Pennsil:

Andreas Sandel
Past:Eccl:Luth: ad Wicaco in Pensylv:

Bibliography

Åberg, Alf. *Karl IX.* Stockholm: Wahlstrom & Widstrand, 1958.

Acrelius, Israel. *Beskrifning Om De Swenska Församlingars Förna och Nävarande Tilstånd Uti Det så kallade Nya Sverige...* Stockholm, 1759

Baptism, Eucharist, Ministry. Faith and Order Paper No. 111. Geneva: World Council of Churches, 1982.

Baar, William H. "Justus Falckner" in 1953 *Yearbook of the United Lutheran Church in America.* F. Eppling Reinartz, ed. Philadelphia United Lutheran Publication House, 1952.

Bergendoff, Conrad. *The Doctrine of the Church in American Lutheranism*, The Knubel-Miller Lectures. Philadelphia: Muhlenberg Press, 1956.

Church Music and Musical Life in Pennsylvania in the Eighteenth Century, Vol. I. The Philadelphia Society of Colonial Dames, 1926.

Clark, Delber Wallace. *The World of Justus Falckner.* Philadelphia: Muhlenberg Press, 1946.

Craig, Peter Stebbins. *The 1693 Census of the Swedes on the Delaware.* Winter Park, FL: SAG Publications, 1993.

Documentary History of the Evangelical Lutheran Ministerium of Pennsylvania and Adjacent States, Proceedings of the Annual Conventions, 1748-1821. Philadelphia: Board of Publication of the General Council of the Evangelical Lutheran Church, 1898.

Ecclesiastical Records of the State of New York. Vol. III. Albany,NY: J. B. Lyon, 1902.

Erler, Georg. *Die jüngere Matrikel der Universität Leipzig, 1559-1909.* Leipzig, 1909.

Falckner, Daniel and Falckner, Justus. Letters translated by George T. Ettinger in *The Pennsylvania German Society,* Vol. 18, Proceedings at Philadelphia, Dec. 8, 1907. Lancaster: New Era Printing Co., 1907.

Flick, Alexander C., ed., *History of the State of New York*, Vol. IX, "Mind and Spirit." New York: Columbia University Press, 1937.

Glatfelter, Charles H. *Pastors and People: German Lutheran and Reformed Churches in the Pennsylvania Field, 1717-1793.* Vol I, "Pastors and Congregations," The Pennsylvania German Society, Breinigsville PA, 1980. Vol. II, "The History," 1981.

Glenn, John G. "The Certificate of Ordination of Justus Falckner" in *The Lutheran Church Quarterly*, Vol. XX, no. 4, October, 1947.

Gloria Dei Records Project. 1646-1786. Peter Stebbins Craig, ed.; Kim Eric Williams, translator. Gloria Dei Church, 916 S. Swanson St., Philadelphia PA 19147-4332.

Heins, Henry H. *Swan of Albany.* First Lutheran Church, Albany NY. Rensselaer NY: Hamilton Printing Co., 1976.

Hudson River Genealogy. Babbage.clarku.edu. "Family of Gerritje Hardik & Rev. Justus Falckner."

Jeyaraj, P. Daniel, "Lutheran Churches in Eighteenth-Century India"in *Lutheran Quarterly,* Vol. XVII, no. 1, Spring 2003.

Johnson, Amandus. *The Swedish Settlements on the Delaware, 1638-1664.* Vols. I & II, Philadelphia, 1911. Republished, Baltimore MD: Clearfield Geneaolgical Publishing Co., 1996.

Jordan, J.P., *The Anglican Establishment in Colonial New York, 1693-1783.* Ann Arbor, MI: University Microfilms, 1973. Ph.D. Thesis, 1971.

Juntke, Fritz, ed. *Matrikel der Martin-Luther-Universität Halle-Wittenberg, 1690-1730.* Part I. Halle, 1960.

Kessler, Martin, translator and ed., *Fundamental Instruction: Justus Falckner's Catechism.* Delhi, NY: ALPB Books, 2003.

Kreider, Harry Julius. *Lutheranism in Colonial New York.* Ann Arbor, MI: Edwards Brothers, 1942. Ph.D. Thesis, Columbia University.

Kreider, Harry Julius with Hart, Simon, *Lutheran Church in New York and New Jersey, 1722-1760.* Pub. by the United Lutheran Synod of New York and New England. Ann Arbor, MI. Edwards Brothers, 1962.

Kreider, Harry Julius. *The Beginnings of Lutheranism in New York.* Gettysburg, PA Times and News Publishing Co., 1949.

Kyrko-Lag och Ordnung, som then Stormägtigste Konung och Herre, HERR CARL den Elofte Åhr 1686 hafwer låtit författa och Åhr 1687 af trycket Utgå och publiceren.... Stockholm: Kongl. Tryckeriet & nya uplagd, 1761.

Lehmann, Helmut T. "The 275th Anniversary of Justus Falckner's Ordin-Ation," in *The Periodical.* Published by the Lutheran Historical Society of Eastern Pennsylvania. Vol. 25, No. 2, March, 1981.

Lohse, Frederick Arthur. *Neuen Sächsischen Kirchengallerir-Pachorie Langenreinsdorf mit Rudelswalde.* 1904

Martling, Carl Henrik. *Svensk liturgihistoria.* Stockholm: Verbum, 1992

Montgomery, Ingun, ed. *Sveriges Kyrkohistoria, 4, Enhetskyrkans tid.* Stockholm: Verbum, 2001.

Nelson, E. Clifford, ed. *The Lutherans in North America.* Revised edition, Philadelphia: Fortress Press, 1980

Norberg, Otto. *Svenska Kyrkans Mission vid Delaware i Nord-Amerika.* Stockholm: A.V. Carlsons Bokforlags-Aktiebolag, 1893

Norelius, Eric. *De Svenksa Luthreska Församlingarna och Svenskarnas Historia i Amerika.* Andra Bandet. Rock Island, IL: Augustana Book Concern, 1916.

Oldenburg, Mark William. *The Evolution of Rituals in East Coast Lutheranism, 1703-1918.* Doctoral dissertation. Madison, NJ: Drew University, 1992.
.Österlin, Lars. *Churches of Northern Europe in Profile, A Thousand Years of Anglo-Nordic Relations.* Norwich: Canterbury Press, 1995.

Pascoe, C.F. *Two Hundred Years of the SPG, 1701-1901.* London: The Society's Office, 1901.

Pennsylvania German Society. Vol. XIV, at Lebanon, PA, 1903. Lancaster, PA: New Era Printing Co., 1905. Daniel Falckner's "Curieuse Nachricht" translated by Julius F. Sachse.

Pennsylvania German Society, Vol. XXV, at Lancaster. Published by the Society at Philadelphia. Lancaster: New Era Printing Co., 1917. "Pennsylvania—the German Influence in Its Settlement and Development."Part XXVII, "The Diarium of Magister Johannes Kelpius,"with annotation by Julius F. Sachse.

Pritchard, Robert W. *A History of the Episcopal Church.* Harrisburg, PA.: Morehouse Publishing, 1991.

Protocol of the Lutheran Church in New York City, 1702-1750. Translated By Simon Hart and Harry J. Kreider. New York: The United Luthean Synod of New York and New England, 1958.

Sachse, Julius Frederick. *Justus Falckner: Mystic and Scholar, Devout Pietist in Germany, Hermit on the Wissahickon, Missionary on the Hudson.* Philadelphia: New Era Printing Co. for the author, 1903.

Sachse, Julius Frederick. *The German Pietists of Pennsylvania, 1694-1708.* Philadelphia: Published by the author, 1895.

Sachse, Julius Frederick. *The Journal of Johannes Kelpius, Magister of the Hermits on the Ridge in Pennsylvania, 1694-1708.* Philadelphia: photographic reproduction of original Latin text for Historical Society of Pennsylvania, 1893.

Sasse, Herman. *This Is My Body.* Adelaide, South Australia.: Lutheran Publishing House, 1958.

Schell, Ernest. "Hermits of the Wissahickon, Johannes Kelpius and the Chapter of Perfection"in *American History Illustrated,* October, 1981, No. 6, Vol. 16.

Schmauk, Theodore E. *A History of the Lutheran Church in Pennsylvania, 1638-1820.* Philadelphia: General Council Publication House, 1903.

Seidensticker, Oswald. "Johannes Kelpius Diary"and "The Hermits of the Wissahickon" in *Pennsylvania Magazine of History and Biography*. Philadelphia: The Historical Society of Pennsylvania, 1887.

Stolt, Bengt. *Svenska Biskops-Vigningar Från reformationen till våra dagar*. Stockholm: Proprius, 1972.

Strodach, Paul Zeller. "On Vestments for the Clergy"in *Lutheran Church Quarterly*, Vol.XII, July, 1939.

Swedberg, Jesper. *Svecia Nova seu America Illuminata. Thet är Nyja Swerige eller America af Gud then Alrahögste med Evangelii lius nådeligen uplyst. 1727*. Handwritten manuscript at Uppsala University Library.

Tappert, Theodore, and Doberstein, John W., translators, *The Journals of Henry Melchior Muhlenberg*. Vol. 1, Philadelphia: Muhlenberg Press, 1942.

van Laer, Arnold J.F. *The Lutheran Church in New York (1649-1772)*. Records in the Lutheran Church Archives at Amsterdam, Holland. New York: New York Public Library, 1948.

Vesper, Herman F. "Sketch" in *The Book of Names, especially relating to the Early Palatines*. Compiled by Lou D. McWethy. Baltimore: Geneaolgical Publishing Co., 1969.

Wentz, Abdel Ross. "The Ordination Certificate of Justus Falckner" in *Concordia Historical Institute Quarterly*, Vol 41, May, 1968.

Whittier, John Greenleaf. *The Poetical Works of Whittier*. Ed. by Hyatt H. Wagonner. Cambridge edition. Boston: Houghton Mifflin Co., 1975.

Williams, Kim-Eric. *The Eight Old Swedes Churches of New Sweden*. Kalmar Nyckel Museum Institute. Wilmington, DE: New Sweden Centre, 1999.

Zwierlein, Frederick J. *Religion in New Netherland, 1623-1664*. Rochester, NY, 1910. Republished, New York: Da Capo Press, 1971.

Endnotes

[1] Ingun Montgomery, editor, *Sveriges Kyrkohistoria, 4 Enhetskyrkans tid* Stockholm: Verbum, 2001, p. 241

[2] Frederick Arthur Lohse, *Neuen Sächsischen Kirchengallerie-Pachorie Langenreinsdorf mit Rudelswalde,* 1904.

[3] *Ibid.*

[4] *Kirchenbüchern von Langenreinsdorf,* copied from the manuscripts in Germany, and translated by Frederick S. Weiser, 2003. Taufbuch, Nr.12, 1672, page 123. While the entry for Justus is rather spare that for Daniel, Jr. is extensive: "Daniel, son of Daniel Falckner, pastor here, born into the world 25 November 1666, the 24th Sunday after Trinity in the morning between 8 and 9 o'clock, was baptized the following Wednesday, the 28th November and his baptismal sponsors were the honorable, noble, greatly esteemed and highly revered Herr Daniel Farber, doctor of jurisprudence and princely counsel from Hollstein; the well-honored, highly-esteemed and well-learned Herr Mauritius Gerhard, princely secretary of Hollstein, who had traveled to Vienna at the time on a princely expedition, whose place was taken by the honored, esteemed, and well-learned Herr Daniel Zahmseil, practicing jurist in Zwickau, the honorable, much esteemed, and virtuous lady Dorothea, wife of Herr M[agister] Andreae Ungibauers, Primary Pastor in Münch-Bernsdorff, in whose place she could not appear because of marital obligations, stood the honorable, esteemed, and virtuous lady Margaretha, wife of Herr Gottfried Schuster, pastor in Langen Hessen." (p.118a in the Taufbuch, 1662, Nr.20). It is estimated that Daniel Jr, died about 1744 having retired from the"Raritan Congregation" in Hunterdon County, New Jersey.

[5] Daniel Falckner to August Hermann Francke at Halle, April 16, 1702, translation by George T. Ettinger from a copy in the Staatsbibliotek, National Library, Berlin as found in *The Pennsylvania German Society, Volume 18, Proceedings at Philadelphia, December 8, 1907,* p.15.

[6] Augustus Lutheran Church in Trappe, Pa., built by Henry Melchior Muhlenberg in 1745 was named for him. It is considered the oldest unaltered Lutheran church building in the United States.

[7] Delber Wallace Clark, *The World of Justus Falckner.* Philadelphia: Muhlenberg Press, 1946, p. 5.

[8] Georg Erler, *Die jüngere Matrikel der Universität Leipzig, 1559-*1909 Leipzig: 1906, reprinted, 1976, p.99

[9] Fritz Juntke, ed. *Matrikel der Martin-Luther-Univerisität Halle-Wittenberg, 1690-1730, Part 1,* Halle, 1960, p.141.

[10] Montgomery, op. cit., p. 181.

[11] Georg Erler, *op. cit.,* p..99.

[12] *Kirchenbüchern von Langenreinsdorf*. "Christian Falckner in 1658 on 5 November at 8:00 p.m. with the Invocation of the Name of Jesus died blessedly. Burial on 8 November. Funeral conducted by Rev. Dominus Paulus Schlegel, faithful pastor in Newkirchen. Proclamation of the Word (sermon) by Rev. Dominus Matthaeus Abbas, Pastor and compater in Langenreinsdorf."

"Mrs. Anna Maria, my dear mother and a pillar of my household on account of her prayers, the surviving widow of the late honorable Herr Christian Falckner died on 10 January 1670 in the evening between 8 and 9 o'clock in true faith in her Redeemer, greatly, dearly, and blessedly fell asleep in her 72nd year of age. Funeral ceremonies were held on the following 13 January in a Christian and honorable way with an assembly of many people. Funeral was conducted by Rev. Dominus Balthasar Spitzner, Pastor in Blanckenhayn. Proclamation of the Word by Rev. Dominus Paulus Schlegel, Pastor in Newkirchen."

"Herr Daniel Falckner, Pastor Loci here, buried on 9 April 1674."

[13] Clark, *op. cit.*, p.14

[14] Clark, *op. cit.*, p. 8

[15] There is no evidence that they were Rosicrucians, as some Masonic historians have alleged.

[16] Clark, op.cit. p.15

[17] Julius Sachse, *The German Pietists of Provincial Pennsylvania, 1694-1708*. Philadelphia: published by the author, 1895, p.391.

[18] *Ibid.*, p.70 ff. The exact location is unknown although the City of Philadelphia has a "Hermit Lane" in Roxborough adjoining the supposed area above the Wissahickon Creek.

[19] *Ibid.,* p.106 ff.

[20] *Church Music and Musical Life in Pennsylvania in the Eighteenth Century*, Vol.I, 1926: The Philadelphia Society of Colonial Dames of America. p.7

[21] That is, Jacob Boehme (1575-1624), famous Lutheran mystic.

[22] John Greenleaf Whittier, *The Poetical Works of Whittier*, edited by Hyatt H. Waggoner, Cambridge Edition. Boston: Houghton Mifflin Company, 1975, p. 106. On the other hand his description of Andreas Rudman as an old white-haired Finn, who sought out Pastorius to converse in Greek and Latin, is totally imaginary.

[23] Clark, *op. cit.*, p. 9.

[24] Julius F. Sachse, *Justus Falckne,r Mystic and Scholar, Devout Pietist in Germany, Hermit on the Wissahickon, Missionary on the Hudson*. Philadelphia: New Era Printing Co. for the author, 1903, pp. 28-29.

[25] Pennsylvania German Society, Vol.XIV (1903).

[26] Sachse, *Justus Falckner, op. cit.*, p.31.

[27] *Ibid.*, pp.38-48

[28] Daniel Falckner to August Francke, April 16, 1702, *op. cit.*, p.13. "My brother performs with me, in outward affairs, what the administration of our authority respecting landed possessions brings with it, and thus, for the time being, he is not fitted for schoolwork." Earlier in the same letter Daniel says that he has already moved to Falckner's Swamp, p. 11. "I have at last received about twenty-five thousand acres in one piece thirty-six miles from Philadelphia; there I have also already begun my residence;..."

[29] Johannes Campanius had a mission to the Indians from 1643-1648 from what is now Chester, Pennsylvania, and John Eliot established his Praying Villages in New England later in the same century, but in each case it was the action of an individual with a missionary zeal rather than the decision of a Church to answer a call for mission that was more than expatriate chaplaincy.

[30] His name seems to have been reversed to Reorus Torkillus. Such a last name is not known, while the first name Torkil is a typical old Swedish male name, even with a Latinized form.

[31] Amandus Johnson, *The Swedish Settlements on the Delaware, 1638-1664*, Volume II, Philadelphia, 1911, republished, Baltimore, Md.: Clearfield, Genealogical Publishing Company, 1996, p.668.

[32] Peter S. Craig, *The 1693 Census of the Swedes on the Delaware.* Winter Park, Fla.: SAG Publications, 1993.

[33] *Kyrko Lag och Ordnung.* Stockholm: Johan Georg Sheidt, 1686. Kap.20, parts 1-3.

[34] Ingun Montgomery, *op.cit.,* p.244.

[35] Alf Åberg, *Karl XI.* Stockholm: Wahlström & Widstrand, 1958, pp.158-160."The view of the Church which the King confessed was dogmatic. God had given the King the power, and those who sought to reduce the King's power thereby violated the divine order. Where there was no wise and exalted King, the people were lost like a ship without a navigator...the King was often portrayed in sermons as a Solomon in a northern Israel. In the same way that all governmental power was concentrated in his hands, he was also the highest authority in the church. He alone had the right to appoint bishops...the King was the church's highest Guardian." Translation: Kim-Eric Williams

[36] Montgomery, op. cit., p.55 and pp.156-157.

[37] *Svecia Nova seu America Illuminata, Thet är Nyja Swerige eller America af Gud then Alrahögste med Evangelii lius nådeligen uplyst. Beskrifwen och utgifwen af Thess och Skara Stifts Biskop D. Jesper Swedberg åhr 1727.* The citation, found in a copy at the Uppsala University Library as a marginal note at paragraph 226, entitled "Rudman's fame and zeal" reads: " Magister Rudman was now ready to

travel home to Sweden, but was prevailed upon to come and put in order a Dutch Lutheran Church in New York, since among other languages he was rather fluent in Dutch. He went there and with great blessings put the congregation in order, as well as to Albany, which was a good distance from there. As he was considering his return trip to Sweden and leaving his congregation in Wiccacow [Vicaco/Philadelphia] in good condition, he approved a German by the name of Justus Falck[ner], who allowed himself to be thus convinced. For Magister Rudman had been charged by Blessed Archbishop Swebilius to ordain someone as a priest if it were necessary. This did indeed happen in the year 1703 on the 24th of November in a public service, held by the Swedish priests in Wiccacow. At this Dean Biörck preached on these words, "How can they preach unless they are sent?"[marginal note Romans 10:15] And thus Falcknen[Falckner] was made available by Magister Rudman, and nothing except blessings and progress was heard about his [ministry in] Office." Translation: Kim-Eric Williams. Actually Björk was not a dean then but became one after Rudman died and retained the title in Sweden at the date of this writing.

[38] Israel Acrelius, *Beskrifning Om De Swenska Församlingars Forna och Närvarande Tilstånd, Uti Det så kallade Nya Sverige...* Stockholm, 1759. Part 5, chapter 1, pp. 12-13.

[39] Bengt Stolt, *Svenska Biskops-Vigningar från reformationen till våra dagar*, Stockholm: Proprius, 1972. p.46.

[40] *Ibid.,* p.47.

[41] Charles H. Glatfelter, *Pastors and People: German Lutheran and Reformed Churches in the Pennsylvania Field, 1717-1793*, Volume 13, The Pennsylvania German Society, Breinigsville, Pa.,: 1981, p.60.

[42] Gloria Dei Records Project, Peter S. Craig, editor, Kim-Eric Williams, translator. Letters, 1697-1702, p. 4a. Translation from Dutch by Robert Naborn.

[43] Gloria Dei Records Project, Peter S. Craig, editor, Kim-Eric Williams, translator, Letters, 1697-1702, p.4. Used by permission. The German original begins: *"Rudman du armen Schweden Hirte, Kam hier ins land zu rechter zeit..."*

[44] Gloria Dei Records Project, Peter S. Craig, editor, Kim-Eric Williams, translator. Letters, 1697-1702, pp. 6-8. Used by permission.

[45] Sachse, *Justus Falckner, op. cit.,* pp. 53-54

[46] *Ibid..,* p.55

[47] Gloria Dei Records Project. Peter S. Craig, editor, Kim Eric Williams, translator. Letters 1697-1702, p.3. Used by permission. Heilsburg is outside of today's, Kaliningrad (Königsburg).

[48] In *Kyrko Lag och Ordning* (Stockholm: Johan Georg Eberdt, 1686), part XVII, "Everything that is written above and all of our decrees about

Bishops should also be applied to Superintendents, who stand with them in the same duty and Office." Translation, Kim-Eric Williams

[49] Lars Österlin, *Churches of Northern Europe in Profile, A Thousand Years of Anglo-Nordic Relations*, Norwich: The Canterbury Press, 1995, pp.82-83.

[50] Gloria Dei Records Project,. Peter S. Craig, editor, Kim-Eric Williams, translator. Letters 1697-1702, p.3. Used by permission.

[51] Auren later retracted his literalistic Sabbatarianism, and with Björck's approval served the Church at Swedesboro, N.J., until his death in 1713; cf. Kim-Eric, Williams, *The Eight Old Swedes Churches of New Sweden*, Wilmington, Del.: New Sweden Centre, Kalmar Nyckel Institute, 1999.

[52] Gloria Dei Records Project, Peter S.Craig, editor, Kim-Eric Williams, translator, , Letters, 1697-1702, pp. 6-8. From Rudman to the Archbishop, 16 June 1702. Tolstadius succeeded in purchasing land in Swedesboro and erected a log church in 1705. After he had been under indictment by the Burlington Court for fathering a child by a maid in the congregation, he apparently committed suicide in the Delaware River in 1706. See: *Swedish Colonial News*, Volume 2, Number 7, Fall, 2000, "The Swedish Church at Swedesboro" by Peter S. Craig.

[53] Sachse, *Justus Falckner*, op. cit., p.59.

[54] Gloria Dei Records Project, Peter S. Craig, editor, Kim-Eric Williams, translator. Gloria Dei Church Book, Sandel narrative I, p.14. Used by permission.

[55] Gloria Dei Records Project, Peter S. Craig,. Editor, Kim-Eric Williams, translator. Published separately in *Swedish Colonial News*, Volume 2, Number 1, Winter, 2000 p.3. Used by permission.

[56] *Ibid.*

[57] Andreas Sandel's commentary on the *klockare* Jonas, refers to Jonas Bjurström, who had come with the first three priests in 1697 as a servant and who remained and married in the colony.

[58] Jesper Svedberg, *Svecia Nova* 16, 170-71, paragraph 79. Manuscript at Uppsala University Library.

[59] Sachse, *Justus Falckner*, *op. cit.*, p. 64.;

[60] Montgomery, op. cit., a special chapter on "Spiritual Songs and Music" is found on pp.280-289. Women sat on the left side of the center aisle and men on the right as one faces the altar. The only remnant of this tradition seems to be the bride standing to the left of the groom in today's marriage ceremonies, although occasional ethnic enclaves preserve this custom.

[61] Gloria Dei Records Project, Peter S. Craig, editor, Kim-Eric Williams, translator. "Andreas Rudman, America's First Hymnist," 2002.Used by permission.

[62] The actual word is *prästskjorta,* "priest's shirt" an archaic word that today would have been *mässhocke.*p.1, Rudman Accounts. The same Cash Book, p.29, Lidman-Eneberg-Falk Accounts, Anno 1731, records a burglary in the sacristy showing only that the "white albs (mässskjortor)" had been stolen. Thus albs were still in use then and were valuable because of their linen.

[63] Thus Sachse's supposition that a chasuble was given to Falckner at his Ordination is without historical background and the window at First Lutheran Church in Albany, based on Sachse's description is a fantasy.

[64] *Protocol of the Lutheran Church in New York City, 1702-1750.* Translated by Simon Hart and Harry J. Kreider. Published by the United Lutheran Synod of New York and New England, New York:1958. p.[43].

[65] Gloria Dei Records Project, Peter S. Craig, editor, Kim-Eric Williams, translator. Gloria Dei Church book, Sandel Narrative 1, p.9. Used by permission. It is also possible that the churchwardens would have attended: Elias Tay, John Rambo, Giösta Giöstason, Petter Bengson and Hans Laican. Sandel Narrative I, p.10. Sachse's supposition about Junior and Senior Church wardens is an Anglican imposition without merit.

[66] Liturgical portions translated by Kim-Eric Williams from the text of the 1571 Church Order photocopy found at the Archives of the Metropolitan New York Synod, Evangelical Lutheran Church in America at Wagner College, Staten Island, N.Y. and an original copy of the 1686 Church Order at the Krauth Memorial Library, Lutheran Theological Seminary, Philadelphia. Pa. The order used at Gloria Dei was no doubt primarily that of 1571, since the 1686 order is an emendation of the Laurentius Petri Order. In fact there was considerable opposition to the 1686 Order in the dioceses since it contained such a strong oath to the King.

[67] The proposed long oath of 1686 with its many references to loyalty to the King and his heirs was resisted by the priests and widely either disregarded or shortened until an agreed-upon formula was reached in 1811. While there was no prescribed oath in the 1571 Order, some oath was used and in this case probably used by Falckner because of its confessional specificity and ministerial descriptiveness in a land with no one religious pattern. The following Oath, proposed by the author, is a shortened form of the one prescribed in 1686, removing all royal references.

[68] *Holy Bible, Revised Standard Version* New York: Thomas Nelson & Sons, 1952.

[69] The usual meetings of the Swedish District/ Ministerium /*Kontrakt* invariably included the Eucharist for this reason.

[70] *Baptism, Eucharist, Ministry.* Faith and Order Paper No. 111, Geneva: World Council of Churches, 1982, p.30, B- 41 "The Act of Ordination."

[71] The Lutheran reformer Olaus Petri retained only the Easter Preface giving the Church of Sweden a unique paschal emphasis at each Eucharist, using the order of Luther's *Formula Missae*, "Sursum Corde" "Easter Preface" "Words of Institution" "Sanctus" "Lord's Prayer" "Pax" "Agnus Dei." The text is in Kim-Eric Williams, "A Brief History of the Swedish Eucharistic Tradition" in *The Bride of Christ*, Pentecost, June, 2001, Vol. XXV, No.3.

[72] RSV; the reference from Bishop Svedberg is found in *Svecia Nova seu America Illuminata*. Cf. above

[73] Abdel Ross Wentz, "The Ordination Certificate of Justus Falckner" in *Concordia Historical Institute Quarterly,* Vol. 41, May, 1968, p.65-86.

[74] *Kyrko Lag och Ordning, 1686,* chapter 22, paragraph 3.

[75] Wentz, op. cit. pp.76-81

[76] P. Daniel Jeyaraj, "Lutheran Churches in Eighteenth-Century India" in *Lutheran Quarterly*, Vol. VII, Number 1, Spring 2003, p.85.

[77] Mark William Oldenburg, "The Evolution of Rituals in East Coast Lutheranism, 1703-1918," doctoral dissertation, Madison, NJ: Drew University, 1992., pp. 51-52.

[78] *Documentary History of the Evangelical Lutheran Ministerium of Pennsylvania and Adjacent States, Proceedings of the Annual Conventions, 1748-1821.* Philadelphia: Board of Publication of the General Council of the Evangelical Lutheran Church, 1898. pp 3-8.

[79] Eric Norelius, *De Svenska Lutherska Församlingarnas och Svenskarnas Historia i Amerika, Andra Bandet,* Rock Island, Ill.: Augustana Book Concern , 1916, p.11. The sessions were held in Jefferson Prairie, Clinton, Wis. The Augustana Church continued its corporate existence until 1962 when it became part of the Lutheran Church in America. In an even larger merger, the L.C.A.became the Evangelical Lutheran Church in America in 1988.

[80] The very small and detailed handwriting of Andreas Sandel makes it clear that he was not the author/scribe despite the conclusion of Prof. Willem J. Kooiman of the University of Amsterdam in 1953. At that time the professor did not have access to the original manuscripts of Sandel in the Gloria Dei Church Book. His opinion can be further explored in Abdel Ross Wentz, "The Ordination Certificate of Justus Falckner" in *Concordia Historical Institute Quarterly,* May 1968, Vol. XLI, No. 2, pp.69-70. There is no evidence that Sandel was ever the "Secretary" of the Swedish Ministerium. Indeed while Rudman was Superintendent there were no other officers and no official Ministerium. After Rudman's death in 1708, Björk was appointed Dean and no Superintendent was ever again appointed in America by the Church of Sweden.

[81] "Gift"is a translation of *munere.*

[82] "Initiated by rite into holy orders" is a translation of *rite sacris ordinibus initiatus.*

[83] Sachse, *Justus Falckner, op.cit.*, pp. 74-75, alt. K-E Williams.

[84] *Ibid.*, p. 75.

[85] *Ibid.*, p.80.

[86] *Protocol, op.cit.*, p.[65].

[87] Clark, *op. cit.*, pp.40ff.

[88] *Ibid.*, p.49.

[89] Sachse, *Justus Falckner,op.cit.*,pp. 98,99.

[90] *Ibid.*, pp. 99-103.

[91] A few Native Americans seem to have been baptized by Johan Campanius (1643-1648) either at his glebe in Upland (Chester) or in the church at Tinicum, although no records exist. Before 1708 Jonas Auren in North East, Maryland, seems to have baptized some Native Americans since their remains have been authenticated in the graveyard of St. Mary Anne's Church.

[92] Sachse, *Justus Falckner,op.cit.*, pp. 102-106.

[93] Clark, *op.cit.*, p. 116.

[94] *Ibid.*, pp. 117-118.

[95] J.P. Jordan, *The Anglican Establishment in Colonial New York, 1693-1783.* Ann Arbor, MI: University Microfilms, 1973, Columbia University PhD. Thesis, 1971, p. 112 The act of the Provincial Assembly in 1706 provided that Baptism did not change a slave's legal status.

[96] *Ibid,* p. 96

[97] *Ibid,* p. 66.

[98] *Ibid,* p. 67.

[99] *The Pennsylvania German Society* Volume 18, Proceedings at Philadelphia, December 8,1907, Lancaster: New Era Printing Co., 1909. translation by Julius F. Sachse, pp. 15 and 17.

[100] Clark, *op.cit.*, pp. 57-58.

[101] Original document in the collection of the Lutheran Historical Society Collection, Library of the Lutheran Theological Seminary, Gettysburg, Pa., from St. James Lutheran Church, Manhattan.

[102] *Lexicon Graeco-Latinum in Novum Domini Nostri Jesu Christi Testamentum,* by Georgio Pasore. London: Jacobus Junius, 1644.

[103] For further discussion of the SPG's lack of support for German ministry, cf. J.P. Jordan, *op.cit.,*p. 112ff.

[104] Arnold J.F.van Laer, *The Lutheran Church in New York, 1649-1772, Records in the Lutheran Church Archives at Amsterdam, Holland.* New York [N.Y.] Public Library, 1948, pp. 98-100.

[105] Gloria Dei Records Project, Peter S, Craig, editor, Kim-Eric Williams, translator. Used by permission. Sandel Narrative I, p. 20 "1706."

[106] vanLaer, *op.cit.*, pp. 103-104.

[107] *Ibid.,* pp.105-106.

[108] *Ibid.,* p. 107.

[109] *Ibid.,* p. 109.

[110] *Ibid.,* p. 110.

[111] Martin Kessler, *Fundamental Instruction: Justus Falckner's Catechism.* Delhi,N.Y.: ALPB Books, 2003, pp. 39-40.

[112] *Protocol, op.cit.*, pp. 16-17.

[113] *Ibid.*, pp. 92-93.

[114] Kessler, *op.cit.*, p. 91.

[115] Hermann Sasse, *This Is My Body*, Adelaide, South Australia: Lutheran Publishing House, 1958. p. 248.

[116] *Ibid.,* p. 100

[117] *Ibid.,* p. 104

[118] *Protocol, op.cit.*, p. [8].

[119] Alexander C. Flick, *History of the State of New York*, Volume IX, "Mind and Spirit." New York: Columbia University Press, 1937. p. 127.

[120] Rudman died on September 17, 1708; cf. Norberg, *Svenska Kyrkans Mission.* p. 27. Eric Björck had given this report to Bishop Jesper Svedberg from Christina (Wilmington, Del.) on July 5, 1708. "Some more news has just come in about Magister Rudman's work as Superintendent. I know that though he would have been satisfied with a lesser title, it drove him, or haunted him to improve himself to more than that which I have now attained; for in truth he has a difficult work. For even if he has learned the English language more completely than me in usual conversation, it still is not his native language. He is not only faithfully appreciated in Philadelphia [Christ Church], but also has charge of a newly-erected congregation [Trinity, Oxford]. He must take care of horses and of each congregation equally, but if he doesn't get help soon, his life and strength will be quite exhausted..." From *Register till Skara Domkapitels Protokoll,* Skara Läns och Stiftsbibliotek.

[121] Clark, *op.cit.*, pp. 79-81.

[122] Sachse, *Justus Falckner,* p.90. and Harry J. Kreider, *Lutheranism in Colonial New York.* Ann Arbor, MI: Edwards Brothers Inc., 1942. PhD. Dissertation for Columbia University., p. 36.

[123] Henry H. Heins, *Swan of Albany.* First Lutheran Church, Albany, NY. Rensselaer, NY: Hamilton Printing Co., 1976, p. 38.

[124] Clark, *op.cit.*, p. 98.

[125] Clark, *op.cit.*, pp. 90-92.

[126] *Ibid.,* p. 97.

[127] Protocol, *op.cit.,* pp [48-49]

[128] *Ibid.,* pp. 99-106.

[129] *Ibid.,* p. 102.

[130] *Ecclesiastical Records of the State of New York,* Vol.III. Albany, N.Y.: J. B. Lyon, 1902, p. 1862.

[131] Clark, *op.cit.,* p 106.

[132] *Ibid.,* p. 112.

[133] *Ibid.,* p. 122.

[134] *Ibid.,* pp. 123-124.

[135] *Ibid.,* pp. 145-146; 148.

[136] *Ibid.,* pp. 148-149.

[137] Jordan, *op.cit.,* p. 223.

[138] Society for the Propogation of the Gospel, *Letter Series, 1705-1710.* Washington: Library of Congress, microfilm.

[139] C.F. Pascoe, *Two Hundred years of the SPG, 1701-1901.* London: The Society's Office, 1901.

[140] Kreider, *Lutheranism in Colonial New York., op.cit.,* p. .35.

[141] *Year Book,* Holland Society, 1903, pp. 49, 57.

[142] Wilhelm C. Berkenmeyer , the successor (1725-1751) of Justus Falckner, relates these details about the alcoholism of Daniel, Jr., to The Very Rev. Friedrich Winckler, Senior of the Lutheran Ministerium of Hamburg in a letter of September 24, 1731: "He was helped into the ministry by the same [Anthony Jacob]Henkel who ordained our Van Dieren. Already at that time his offensive life was so abominable to his own sainted brother [Justus Falckner] that even on his deathbed the latter warned his whole parish not to have anything to do with this drunkard. But although the late [Justus] Falckner said this because he was urged by his conscience, I still must admit that he made out the call to his brother, which the latter is showing off. Before I came to this country, he used to visit and minister to our parish, but he abased himself everywhere so that several times he almost fell from the pulpit…He even annoys women on the street, and is sometimes found sleeping on the side of the road with the brandy keg on his back." Equally disturbing is the description of Anna Maria Schuchartin, Daniel's wife. "…she has not yet forgotten her former devilish tricks, even though she has lost her wits and mind through drunkenness…A man from Hamburg, Gustav Rull, who lived in Falckner's home for half a year to study medicine under him, told me privately that he [Daniel] was like an angel compared to her." From Simon Hart and Harry J. Kreider, *Lutheran Church in New York and New Jersey, 1722-1760, op.cit.,*pp. 17, 19. If we are to believe this report from Berkenmeyer, that Anthony Henkel ordained Daniel, Jr., then the latter would be the next in line of Lutheran ordinands in America. No other evidence for this has appeared except for the fact that Henkel was the pastor for the congregation at Falckner's Swamp/New Hanover where

Daniel was the real estate agent, and that Berkenmeyer does not question the legitimacy of his ordination. His alcoholism may also explain why he had to give up his work at Falckner's Swamp and move to New Jersey.
[143] Charles H. Glatfelter, *Pastors and People: German Lutheran and Reformed Churches in the Pennsylvania Field, 1717-1793, op.cit.,* p. 209.
[144] *Ibid.,* p.208.
[145] Clark, *op.cit.,* pp. 156-157.
[146] Clark, *op.cit.,* p. 147 from the Kocherthal Marriage records.
[147] *Ibid.,* pp. 160-161.
[148] *Ibid.,* p. 159.
[149] Hudson River Genealogy, babbage@clarku.edu, "Family of Gerritje Hardick (75) & Rev. Justus Falckner; #239, Anna Catharina, #240, Sara Justa.
[150] *Ibid.,* #241.
[151] The exact location is uncertain, except that it would be across from today's Athens and about two miles north of Hudson, NY.
[152] Clark, *op.cit.,* pp. 168-170.
[153] *Ibid.,* p.171.
[154] *Protocol,* p.[6], July 3, 1708, "…Mr. Van de Burgh shall pay to the deacons what he is in arrears on the Pastor's salary."
[155] Harry J. Kreider and Simon Hart, *Lutheran Church in New York and New Jersey, 1722-1760, op.cit.,* p.1.
[156] *Ibid.,* p. 175.
[157] *Ibid.,* pp. 153-155; 159, 164-165.
[158] Van Laer, Arnold, J.F. *The Lutheran Church in New York (1649-1772) op.cit.,* p.111.
[159] Clark, *op.cit.,* p. 168.
[160] *Ibid.,* p. 171
[161] *Ibid.,* pp. 171-172.
[162] *Protocol. op.cit.,* p.49, "Packet 13," Inventory list.
[163] Jordan, *op.cit.,* p. 223.
[164] *Protocol, op.cit.,* p. [88-89]
[165] Sachse, *Justus Falckner, opcit.,* p.134. (alt. The original word "priest" is re-supplied.)
[166] The Ministerium of Pennsylvania was organized in 1748 but the Ministerium of New York was not organized until 1786.
[167] The translation calls him "Mr. Hinckler, living about Manatanien." The footnote on page 134 misidentifies him as Gerhard Henkell.
[168] *Ibid.,* p. 137 (alt.)
[169] Glatfelter, *op.cit.,* Vol.II, "The History," p.31. The congregation was Reeds Church, today Zion-St.John's in Stouchburg, Pa.
[170] *Protocol, op.cit.,* p. [250]

[171] *The Journals of Henry Melchior Muhlenberg,* translated and edited by Theodore Tappert and John Doberstein. Philadelphia: Muhlenberg Press, 1942, Volume 1, p. 237.

[172] Glatfelter, *op,cit.,* Vol. I, "Pastors and Congregations", p. 65.

[173] Clark, *op.cit,* pp. 161-162. After the name Kocherthal on his memorial stone, the name "Hereschias" is also mentioned. In Nelson, ed., *The Lutherans in North America,* Theodore Tappert documents that Kocherthal's family name was Harrsch (p. 14, n. 49).

[174] Kreider and Hart, *Lutheran Church in New York and New Jersey, 1722-1760, op.cit.,* p. 9.

[175] *Ibid.,* pp. 161, 174.

[176] Jordan, *op.cit.,* p. 223.

[177] Kreider, *Lutheranism in Colonial New York, op.cit.,* p. 37.

[178] New York City Surrogate Office, proved January 11 (Julian) or January 22 (Gregorian).

[179] Account of Johannes Sybrandt, translated by Peter Christoph, 2003.

[180] Rudman's hymns have been translated and set to appropriate tunes by the Gloria Dei Records Project. Some of the hymns of Kelpius have been translated and published by Robert E. Bornemann, former professor at the Lutheran Seminary in Philadelphia.

[181] Sachse, *Justus Falckner, op.cit.,* p. 18.

[182] *The Holy Bible, Revised Standard Version.* New York: Thomas Nelson & Sons, 1952.

[183] Sachse, *Justus Falckner, op.cit.,* p. 20.

[184] *Ibid.,* p. 21.

[185] *Ibid.*

[186] *Protocol, op.cit.,* p.[250] Letter to the Swedish Lutheran pastors in Pennsylvania, November 5,1734.

[187] Jehu Curtis Clay, *Annals of the Swedes on the Delaware.* Philadelphia, Pa..: J. C. Pechin, 1835, p. 86.

[188] Bengt Stolt, *Svenska Biskops-Vigningar från reformationen till våra dagar.* Stockholm: Proprius, 1972, p. 102.

[189] *The Doctrine of the Church in American Lutheranism,* The Knubel-Miller Lectures. Philadelphia: Muhlenberg Press, 1956.

[190] From an undated letter in the archives of the Lutheran Theological Seminary, Gettysburg, Pa., as quoted in note 81, *The Periodical,* Vol.25, No.2, March 1981, published by Lutheran Historical Society of Eastern Pennsylvania, from a lecture by Helmut T. Lehmann, given on April 22,1978, "The 275th Anniversary of Justus Falckner's Ordination."

[191] Undated manuscript owned by Zion Lutheran Church, Athens, NY.

[192] It has been republished in New York by AMS Press, 1970.

[193] Theodore E. Schmauk, *A History of the Lutheran Church in Pennsylvania, 1638-1820*. Philadelphia: General Council Publication House, 1903. He was a parish pastor, literary editor for *The Lutheran*, President of the General Council and an adjunct professor at the Lutheran Seminary at Philadelphia.

[194] A biography of Sachse is found in *Pennsylvania German Society*, meeting at Ephrata, 1920, Vol.XXI. Meadville, Pa.: The Tribune Publishing Co., 1925.

[195] *Justus Falckner,*. A 250th Anniversary pamphlet for Zion Lutheran Church, Athens, NY, 1953.

[196] Paul Zeller Strodach, *On Vestments for the Clergy*, in *Lutheran Church Quarterly*, Vol.XII, July, 1939, p. 315.

[197] Clark, *op.cit.,* p. 37.

[198] *Ibid.*, p. 47.

[199] William H. Baar, "Justus Falckner" in the *1953 Yearbook of the United Lutheran Church in America*. F. Eppling Reinartz, editor. Philadelphia: United Lutheran Publication House, 1952, p. 8.

[200] Mark William Oldenburg, *The Evolution of Ordination Rituals in East Coast Lutheranism, 1703-1918*. Ann Arbor, Mich: U.M.I., 1992, Drew University, p. 29.

[201] Helmut T. Lehmann, "The 275th Anniversary of Justus Falckner's Ordination" in *The Periodical*. Published by the Lutheran Historical Society of Eastern Pennsylvania, Vol. 25, No.2, March, 1981.

[202] *Baptism, Eucharist, Ministry*, *op.cit.,* p. 22, #13, "Responsibility of Ordained Ministry."